CD-DVF-688

THE FUTURE OF RELIGION

THE FUTURE OF RELIGION

James O. Unwin

Exposition Press   *New York*

FIRST EDITION

© 1973 by James O. Unwin

SBN 0-682-47605-6

Manufactured in the United States of America

Published simultaneously in Canada by Transcanada Books

Contents

One

Introduction

This book attempts a rigorous comparison and clarification of religious differences that exist between Jews and Christians. This task is approached with full awareness by the author that it is impossible to encompass in any book all aspects of Christian belief as such exist today. And so this book deals primarily with the Medieval Christian beliefs which are the basis of modern Christian belief, even though many millions who call themselves Christians do not accept these basic beliefs.

The author, who was raised and educated a Roman Catholic, has been led, in his consideration of these religious differences, to the conclusion that there is no validity to the Christian departure from Judaism: that there is no validity to the Medieval basic Christian beliefs and no validity to modern Christian belief.

It is well known that those who are of the persuasion of one or another of the denominations of the Judeo-Christian religious heritage "differ on fundamentals." The Jew and the Christian can each read the same chapter or verse of the Bible and each will derive a different meaning from it, because the same words have different meanings in the different persuasions. If each attempts to define his words and meanings, he must define his definitions and his definitions of his definitions and perhaps define the word "define." In this book the author has avoided this problem and achieved clarification by limiting the consideration of religious differences to those concepts of the Hebrew and Christian religions that have a mathematically expressible definition and what follows from these definitions. (No one should be frightened from reading further by this abstruse-sounding introduction, because the discussion is not that complex.)

This limitation clarifies the religious difference because such definitions are rigorous and are defined by mathematics. Therefore neither party to the religious difference can have his own definition. Nor can either side accuse the other of a bigoted understanding of the definition, because it is impossible to have a bigoted understanding of a mathematical concept. Another reason the religious difference is clarified is that all those who claim to be Jewish or Christian agree on these definitions and the truths of mathematics: Thus no one "differs on fundamentals" from anyone else on these fundamental truths of mathematics. True dialogue is attained.

The most important advantages to this approach are that the religious differences can be understood by limiting consideration to these concepts, and that each party to the religious difference can use the other party's concepts with the same confidence one uses the concepts of mathematics in daily living. Also, this text can be translated from one language to another with that same precision of meaning as any other text on mathematics.

One pair of mathematically expressible definitions is considered per chapter. The Hebrew and counterpart Christian definition are each clarified, compared, and related to their respective biblical texts. Likely reasons for the differences are set forth. Then we consider what it means in terms of these mathematically expressible concepts that Christians believe the Hebrew religion was valid until Christ's time, that Christ practiced the Hebrew religion, and then set it aside and so on. The differences that follow in the religious and political spheres from the mathematically expressible differences are also compared.

Of these concepts only one, infinity, is a mathematical concept. The other are religious concepts that can be defined mathematically.

What emerges from this comparison, as the following pages will show, is, first, that the concepts of Judaism are very familiar to all English-speaking peoples, but not as Judaism: as a religion contradictory to Christianity. This familiarity exists because these peoples have freely borrowed concepts over the centuries from the Hebrew Bible (which Christians call the Old Testament) and have subjected these concepts to an enormous amount of development. However, Christians have monumentally ignored Judaism and the part these same concepts serve in that religion.

Second, what emerges is a qualification of above statements. Christians and Jews agree on definitions of mathematical concepts and on the truths of mathematics, except in the religious sphere and in spheres influenced by religion. The concepts of the Christian religion that have a mathematical expression are found herein to be concepts of Roman numeral mathematics. This is probably to be expected because the early Christians for the most part used Roman numerals. The mathematically expressible concepts of the Hebrew religion are found to be in agreement with the ancient Hebrew mathematics which is conceptually the same as Arabic numerals.

Third, what emerges is that these mathematically expressible concepts are concepts of central importance in each of the two religions and are central to the religious difference. Christianity is Judaism passed through the minds of a celibate clergy headed by an absolutist monarchical, religious-political authority, the Medieval Papacy. The concepts of Judaism herein are those that serve the purposes of the Jewish common man, and common men everywhere who have heard about these concepts. In Christianity these same concepts are believed to have evolved into concepts that, in effect, serve the purposes of this absolutist religious-political authority and that now serve the purposes of absolute rulers everywhere.

Two

Infinity Becomes Limited

The first mathematically expressible concept to be considered is infinity. In both the Hebrew and Christian religions, God is understood to be infinite, but the Christian concept of infinity has a visible limited aspect that contradicts the Hebrew. In Christianity, God is everywhere but became limited and visible in the body of Jesus Christ, in the three Persons of the Trinity, in the Eucharistic bread and wine, and in the risen Christ. If God is already everywhere, how he can be limited and visible in Christ's body is unexplainable. And how can the doctrine of the Real Presence limit Him to a piece of bread or make Him any more present in bread and wine? If God is infinite, how can He be three limited entities, Persons? Three limited entities cannot add up to infinity. Christ, as God, is believed to be infinite, but His limited entity, His body, is seen as reproducible, in unlimited fashion, in the Eucharistic bread and wine. This is a concept of infinity that in modern mathematics would be inherently contradictory and therefore invalid because of these visible and limited aspects.

The Hebrew concept of an infinite God differs from the Christian in that it has no visible limited aspect and is in agreement with the modern concept of infinity. It holds that "Nothing can be known about God, but here are His Laws" (referring to the Ten Commandments), and "He is known by his Laws," which are the words of Moses. We can understand today that an infinite Being cannot be comprehended by man, which is why nothing can be known about Him. Also, the second Commandment says, "Thou shalt erect no graven image of God." We again can understand today that no graven image of God can

11

be, because God is infinite. No image of God could be infinite, therefore there can be no valid graven image of God. God cannot become man or be present in bread and wine, Christ cannot be God, and there cannot be three Persons in God because these beliefs are violations of the Graven Image Commandment. If it is idolatry for the Hebrews to worship a brazen calf, then it is idolatry also to worship a man who says he is God or to worship a piece of bread. The God of the Hebrews speaks to men from a burning bush or from behind a cloud and does not take human or other limited form because He is infinite and therefore cannot be limited. The Hebrew Bible does not say directly that God is infinite in the modern mathematical sense, because the Hebrew language and mathematical knowledge of that day were not sufficiently developed to carry this meaning.

Jews have maintained their understanding of their infinite God from the times of Abraham and Moses to the present day. Recognizing that Christ was a Jew and that the Apostles and Disciples of Christ were Jews, what might account for the development of the conceptual differences in Christianity that we have defined above? The difference could have arisen from understanding the Hebrew statement, "Nothing can be known about God . . ." and viewing Christianity as new revealed truth. But this mathematically expressible 'new revealed truth' cannot be reconciled with the old revealed truth. Thus the difference is more likely to have arisen by later followers understanding the Hebrew concept of an infinite God in terms of Roman numeral mathematics.

As will be seen repeatedly in the following chapters, the Christian mathematically expressible concept in each case differs from its Hebrew counterpart as Roman numeral mathematics differs from Arabic numeral mathematics and the modern mathematics that has been built on it. Roman numerals are a mathematical system by picture writing. To write two, three, or four, one draws a picture of II, III, or IIII sticks, fingers, or lines side by side. There is no zero in Roman numerals because one cannot draw a picture of what zero represents: nothing. To draw a picture of something is to delimit it or delineate it: to draw a line around it. Within this mathematical system how does one conceive the infinite, the unlimited? Here the system breaks down. It cannot picture the unlimited because the unlimited cannot be delimited. The Christian concept of infinity has a limited visible aspect because it is a Roman numeral concept of infinity. Thus God to the Christian is Christ holding the world in His hands. But this is not an infinite God; it is a God only 100,000 miles tall, hardly tall enough to reach the Moon.

The Christian concept of infinity is reproducible in unlimited fashion in the Eucharistic bread and wine because it is a concept of many, or many times many, rather than infinity. The name for one thousand in most languages is derived from the word for many, because people in ancient times did not count up that high very often. Any number beyond one hundred or so was "many."

The Christian concept of the infinite universe is a limited visible one also in agreement with Roman numeral mathematics, limited in time and space, because Christian belief holds that the world will end, at which time the stars will fall from the heavens and so on. It is well known today that all of the stars other than the Sun are too remote to fall to earth and that the universe has existed for many billions of years. The Hebrew universe has no such limitation in time or in space.

And the difference could have arisen by later followers of Christ understanding the Hebrew concepts and the story of Christ as they understood the old Greek and Roman pagan religion—as a new mythology or a new idolatry. In this religion, gods are persons. Mars and Justice are respectively a god bedecked in war clothes and a goddess blindfolded. God became man in paganism as witness the worship of the Roman Emperor as a god. In this religion, the gods also have a dwelling place. Zeus and the Greek gods dwell atop Mt. Olympus. Janus, a two-faced god after whom January is named, dwells at entrances, hence his place as the first month of the year. Ceres, goddess of wheat, dwells in fields that produce good yields and avoids other fields. From this kind of thinking, it is a short step to the understanding that God the Father, the Son, and the Holy Spirit dwell in bread and the spirits of wine; that we should receive Christ into our hearts; that we should believe that the Word became Flesh and dwelt among us; that the Holy Spirit descended on the Apostles and disciples on the first Pentecost; that Christ should dwell within us; that a militaristic spirit is central to Christianity and is expressive of the guidance and presence of the Holy Spirit. All these concepts of divinity are contradictory to the Hebrew concept of an infinite God who is already everywhere in a way we cannot know.

The religious difference could have arisen simply by translating the Bible into Latin, because Latin words are in agreement with Roman numeral concepts and concepts of the old mythology.

We can express the religious difference by saying that the New Testament concept of infinity is the old one from Roman numerals, whereas the Old Testament concept of infinity is the new one in agreement with modern mathematics.

In the light of this clarification, let us consider certain Christian beliefs.

1.   Before Christ, these are the alternative Christian beliefs:

a) The Hebrew religion was valid. God was unlimited invisibly infinite as Jews understand him to be. Both religions are in agreement on this matter.

b) The Hebrew religion was valid but God was limited visibly infinite as Christians understand Him but was not revealed as such. However, Jews have not understood Him as such because of the Graven Image Commandment. This Christian position ignores this Commandment and therefore requires that the Hebrew religion never to have been valid. It makes Christ's practice of the Hebrew religion baseless and nonsensical. This Christian belief holds that a valid religion has been built on a religion that never was valid. The statement in Genesis, "Let Us make man to Our image," indicates that God has an image, that He is more than one Person, to those Christians who hold this position.

2.   At some point in time, perhaps the birth of Christ, the Christian religion became valid and is valid today.

This belief (together with 1 (a) above) requires that the infinite God of the Hebrews have evolved at that point in time into the limited infinite God of the Christians. And as He so evolved, the universe He created supposedly evolved into one limited in space and time, a universe to be destroyed by an Apocalyptic end of the world. But the universe did not so evolve, except in the minds of Christians, because modern science tells us that the universe has remained infinite since before man was on earth. This would indicate that the God of the Hebrews evolved into the limited infinite God of the Christians also only in the minds of Christians. This belief also raises difficult questions as to the Hebrew religion Christ practiced. If Christ became God at birth, or at any time up to the Last Supper, then His worshipping the unlimited infinite God of the Hebrews, when this God no longer exists or never did exist, is nonsensical. Or if Christ became God the day He was crucified the King of the Jews, he is again the leader of an invalid religion.

Why would this evolution of God take place? To say that God evolved in this fashion as a punishment to the Jews for the "crime of crucifying Christ" is to ignore that this requires God to have evolved before the "crime" was committed. Why would God evolve into something that contradicts Himself—a limited infinite Being?

This clarification also raises difficult questions as to the accuracy of the Gospel account that says Christ revealed His divinity at the Last Supper. If so, why is it that His fellow Jews did not ask why God has violated His Graven Image Commandment? This would be their first question, because prohibitions against such idolatry are a central theme of the Jew's Bible. The

Christian belief in effect says that it was wrong for the Jews to practice idolatry before Christ; it is right afterward.

3.   After Christ, these are the alternative beliefs.

a) The Hebrew religion is still valid but obsolete. This Christian belief would require God to be both unlimited infinite in the Hebrew sense and limited infinite in the Christian sense. And it would hold it right and also obsolete and wrong in the same instant for men to erect a graven image of God. It is clear that both concepts of God cannot be valid because each contradicts the other, and the Christian concept contradicts itself. If the Hebrew understanding is valid today or was ever valid, then the Christian concept cannot be valid, and therefore the Christian concept cannot make the Hebrew concept invalid or obsolete.

b) The Hebrew religion is no longer valid. Christians acknowledge that the Hebrew concept of infinity is valid today because it is utilized in modern mathematics, science, and technology. And they recognize that the Christian concept of limited infinity is inherently contradictory and useless in these same fields. It is nonsensical and mythological. This belief requires that Christians reverse this position in the religious sphere, apparently by keeping a closed mind on the subject and by forcing themselves to believe.

It is obvious that the Hebrew interpretation is far more sensible than the Christian interpretation regarding infinity. Because they have so completely ignored Judaism, Christians are unaware of the predicament that they departed from Judaism to a less sensible, mythological mathematical concept of the infinite God that is inherently contradictory. This mathematically invalid Christian concept has been forced on a valid Hebrew concept, and as we saw above, it does not fit. But what might be the purpose of forcing it? To answer this question, let us consider some of the other differences which follow in the religious sphere from these two concepts of infinity.

As two concepts of an infinite universe. The Hebrew universe is infinite in time and in space. In the Covenant with Noah, whose descendants are all mankind, God agrees that he will never again destroy the world. Thus because men will be on this planet for many thousands or millions of years hence, conservation of natural resources and of the ancient works of man is of great importance. The Christian universe, on the contrary, is limited in time by the "End of the World," when stars in a limited outer space will fall to earth. The idea of a forthcoming "End of the World" was widespread in the United States in the nineteenth century along with equally widespread destruction of natural resources, presumably because all will be destroyed anyhow. Thus a world that will not be destroyed by God, has evolved into a world that will be destroyed.

However, more pertinent to our question, as two concepts of an infinite God, the Christian concept offers authorities an opportunity to dominate whomever they can and to withdraw those dominated from anyone that cannot be dominated, whereas the Hebrew concept offers no such opportunity. And this tells us our reason why the Christian concept has been forced on the Hebrew. Authorities could make God say whatever they want Him to say, by putting the required words into the mouth of Christ. Such as, "On this rock I will build my Church" and "I give to you the keys of the kingdom of Heaven," words understood as authorizing Papal rule. Also, Christ, as limited infinite, creates the concept of a Big Man before whom all other men are little. This concept of the inequality of all men before a big man is basic to all forms of absolutism. Christ is so big that millions can eat of His flesh and drink His blood every Sunday.

On the contrary, authorities did not have an opportunity to change the Hebrew Word of God, because its understanding was held by Jews scattered over the world. The Jews' Bible was not set down in print until between 600 B.C. and A.D. 220 because Jews feared that this would offer to those who could read and write the opportunity to control those who could not by falsifying the text. Given this strong Hebrew tradition against using God or "truth" to dominate people, one could expect Jews to find the Christian concept of God unacceptable. A God who has no image cannot create in men's minds the idea of a big man before whom all other men are little.

God truly present in bread and wine can also be used by authorities to control people by warning of Hell—fire and damnation and/or the end of the world if they do not receive God regularly under these forms, and by requiring them to confess their sins and do penance before receiving Him. The concept can make authorities absolutist dictators over the spiritual life and death of adherents. God would be seen as authorizing such absolutism. No such opportunity is offered by the Hebrew concept of God.

Also, this Christian concept of God dwelling in men through the reception of bread and/or wine and other sacraments offers authorities an opportunity to withdraw men from those the authorities cannot dominate by creating a view of mankind divided into we versus they: those men who think they are morally better because God dwells in them, and those thought to be morally inferior. This concept authorizes the idea of morally better Christians ruling a heathen world, which has been a major theme of Christian imperialists for centuries. The moral inadequacy of non-Christians is expressed as Original Sin, which is erased on being Christened. In Judaism, this indwelling cannot be valid because it is an expression of idolatry, of self-worship, and is contradictory to the Hebrew concept of the equality of all men before God and God's Law.

The infinite God of the Hebrews, because He cannot be limited to the person of Christ, to bread and wine, or to dwelling in men, cannot be used to dominate people. Therefore there is no authority in Judaism to dominate Jews. It has no counterparts to bishops, cardinals, or popes and needs none. Each Jew is a priest. The rabbi is a teacher. He leads because he has superior knowledge, not because he is morally better or it is his right. The Jews as Chosen are understood not to be morally better as such, only chosen to bear the burden of witnessing the truth. Even Hitler admitted that Judaism is based on the moral equality of all men. The Christian sacraments of Penance, Holy Eucharist, and Holy Orders are, therefore, from the Jewish standpoint, abuses of authority institutionalized for so long that they are encrusted with age.

This clarification shows us our first reason why Jews worldwide are in agreement on the essentials of their religion. These essentials are common sense in agreement with the universally accepted truths of mathematics. Our first reason why Christians will never reach a consensus on the essentials of Christianity is that this first essential is not based on common sense: limited infinity is not in agreement with the universally accepted truths of mathematics, nor is it reasonable to say that limited infinity is an improvement on the unlimited infinity of the Jewish concept. This understanding confirms the judgment of those who say the Christian religion is a form of insanity. The Christian position is that the unreasonable belief is an improvement on the reasonable Hebrew belief. Therefore an effect of the Christian belief is to create a thought system in which common sense does not apply. Thus in Christian religious matters men cannot think for themselves and thus they need an authority to tell them what to think. They need to be dominated. Hence, there are today innumerable Christian denominations each centered on an authority.

The Jew and the Christian each read the same Bible. The Jew derives a common sense understanding, as mathematics is common sense, that frees him from control by authority. The Christian apparently suspends his common sense because he reads into the same text the basis by which authorities should rightly dominate him by telling him what to believe. Thus a constitution and a bill of rights is barely workable in many Christian nations, because the Christian has the attitude that, whatever any text actually says, it means the authorities should dominate him.

Because Christians have so completely ignored Judaism, they are unaware of their predicament of considering it an improvement to have made a departure from a religious concept that cannot be used to control people to a concept that can be so used.

Our first mathematically expressible difference is explainable not as a supernatural or mysterious event but simply that the Jewish concept was corrupted by ignorance and by the lust for power present in the Roman world in the first century after Christ. Christian theologians would say that the irreconcilability of Hebrew with Christian beliefs is a mystery since nothing can be known about God, therefore, it cannot be known why or how He can evolve into limited infinity. We shall see that neither this nor any other of these irreconcilables are mysteries. To call them such is to close one's eyes to the uses of religion for the purpose of controlling people.

Politics involves the power to use force within a given territory. These Christian beliefs say something about who should hold this power and how he shall use force. The beliefs say that power should be invested in a big man assisted by party members—all of whom have the right to dominate others, as Christ vested power in Peter and the Apostles. When the top man expires, a new leader will be selected by the group from their number. He will rule for life. The authorities threaten the equivalent of hell-fire and damnation—torture and imprisonment —to those whom they cannot dominate. Subordinates can be required to confess their transgressions and can rightly be subjected to other invasions of privacy to determine if they are loyal. It is right for the authorities to have absolute control over the life and death of individuals. Those who are members of the party in power, that is those who can be dominated most completely, are one class of citizens and those outside it are an inferior class.

These are the very familiar features of twentieth century dictatorship—whether the Latin-American military junta, the Communist Party of Soviet Russia, or the Fascist Parties of Italy, Spain, and Germany. Christians in these nations are impaled on the horns of this dilemma: that if it is right and necessary to be so dominated and withdrawn from others in the religious sphere, then it must be right also in the political sphere. If not, what is the flaw in this line of reasoning?

A religion that manipulates God provides authorization for a political system that does likewise. And this is a characteristic of totalitarians who equate Him with man's "inner voice" ("the voice of blood"). The Providence so often appealed to by Hitler was identified with his will. As the Crusades were God's will: His will was actually the will of the popes.

A religion centered on the worship of a big man, on objects such as bread and wine, on the veneration of priests and saints, and having as its central aspect the indwelling of the Holy Spirit could offer no objection to nationalism as the worship of the nation's leaders, citizenry, its national shrines, and the "father-land." Since it is right to lay down one's life for one's faith in Christ, it must be right to do the same for one's faith in the nation's leaders. Thus in two world wars, soldiers on both sides fought for "God, King, and Country." Judaism would reject all such nationalism as expressions of idolatry.

Three

Abstraction: Law Becomes a Person

The second mathematically expressible concept to be considered is abstraction. Abstraction is a characteristic of all the concepts of modern mathematics. This means that such concepts have no physical existence: they are thoughts. No man or thing can become a mathematical concept. A contradictory concept of abstraction is central to the Christian religion. Abstract concepts such as *word, law* and *truth* have a limited visible physical existence as the Person of Jesus Christ. The Word, which is the Hebrew Law, becomes the Person of Christ, as in the statement in the Nicene Creed, "the Word was made Flesh and dwelt among us." The Hebrew Word or Law is for the most part a statement of self-evident truths. Part of it is stated in the Ten Commandments. It has been passed down orally over the centuries to the present day. The Law in the first five books of the Hebrew Bible is the written part of it for the primitive society of Jews of that day. The political aspects of the Hebrew Law in their modern development are the same as British and American civil and constitutional law, because those Anglo-Saxons who built this law over the centuries borrowed very heavily from a common sense understanding of the law they found in the Bible. This is the same as the Jews' common sense understanding of their Law. Jews the world over are in essential agreement on this meaning of their Law for the same reasons British and Americans are. It is a common sense understanding based on self-evident truths. Long before Christ, the Jewish community had developed ideas on the rights of the accused, the right of trial by jury, and so on.

British and American law in turn presume a citizenry informed by the Law in the Bible. The Magna Carta, widely recognized as the basis of our rights and liberties, is mainly a

23

document recognizing law above the king. Much else need not be said by it because the Law in the Bible says it. The Preamble to the American Constitution in saying, "We hold these truths to be self-evident," is holding other Bible truths, such as those of the Ten Commandments, as so self-evident that it is unnecessary to mention them as such.

Neither the Law in the Bible nor British law contain a bill of rights as such is attached to the United States Constitution. This is because people, whether Jews, Englishmen, or Americans, understand that they have their rights when they become aware of them and exercise them as such. (Because men are endowed by their Creator with these rights.) They do not have to wait until such rights are formalized in a document. Nor do people lose their rights if this document is destroyed. Such is a meaning of "government by the people." Formalizing these rights may obscure recognition of this meaning and thereby offer an opportunity for authorities to control people by limiting their rights.

However, a nation which envisioned itself being populated by vast millions of immigrants, to whom rule of law had previously been only a dream, needed a document to inform these immigrants of their rights. And a nation so large that communications could only spread slowly needed a formal procedure for amending the Constitution. Neither the island of Great Britain nor the Jewish world community have been in a similar position. The United Nations Declaration of the Rights of Man has the same purpose: to inform men of their rights, not to limit their rights.

Judaism has, in turn, been greatly influenced by British and American legal development because, between year 70 of the Christian era and 1948, the Jews had no nation of their own in which to practice the politically relevant concepts of their Law. The influence of this legal devlopment and that of modern science have brought about the Conservative and Reform movements within the religion. Thus many aspects of the Law are now regarded as having served an ancient hygienic purpose and are consequently no longer practiced. Because the Hebrew Law and British and American law are each logical systems based on the same positions, we speak of them as constituting one rational system called the Common law.

The Jewish Law also includes the laws of modern mathematics and science.

The above is how millions of English-speaking Christians have understood the Jewish Law in the political sphere and other nonreligious spheres, in agreement with the Jewish understanding. In Judaism, as well as in British and American law, modern mathematics, and science, this law (Law) remains abstract. It cannot become a person. Moses remains only the lawgiver of the Hebrew Law. He never becomes the Law even though God speaks to him and he speaks it to the Israelites. No English-speaking person thinks that British and American law can become a person who should be worshipped and received under the appearances of bread and wine. Nor does anyone think that the laws of mathematics and science, such as the law of gravity, can become a person either. The idea is absurd, but that is the Christian belief in disagreement with Judaism. Because Christians have so completely ignored Judaism, they are in the predicament of believing this absurdity in accepting the Nicene Creed statement "the Word was made Flesh and dwelt among us."

Christians see only the visible, assumed to be arbitrary, aspects of the Hebrew Law, such as the tablet of the Ten Commandments, the dietary laws, the distinction between clean and unclean animals, the practice of circumcision, the promise of a messiah, etc. In believing that the Word was made Flesh, Christians believe that these assumed arbitrary aspects of the Word become Flesh in Christ, Who authorized to be instituted new arbitrary religious observances. However, these visible aspects are tied to the invisible concepts of rights and liberties of Judaism in one rational legal system: Christians are saying that they believe rights and liberties also became flesh in Christ but they don't realize this. And we shall see that this is the actual understanding attached to this belief. The belief in effect makes inalienable rights and liberties into a Man who will decide what these are for all men. And the belief makes such rights and liberties into a piece of bread which can be granted or withheld from the communicant by religious authorities.

Thus, at the Vatican II Ecumenical Council, bishops had to petition the pope and the council as a whole for a declaration on human rights, because such rights and liberties had become flesh in the Vicar of Christ. But the point is that the Word cannot become Flesh and this Council was a sham, an exercise in pomposity and arrogance.

It is obvious that the Christian belief has nothing to do with the Hebrew understanding. The belief can be illustrated by a ludicrous example. It is as if a Hebrew rule, twelve inches in length, called the foot, is believed to have evolved into something with toes, toenails, ankle, heel, instep, and so on. The abstract foot became personified, for the purpose of holding people down (by stepping on them?). Since then, arguments have ensued as to which authority's foot will rule. The Christian belief is a play on words for a purpose.

Having defined this religious difference that has a mathematical expression, we should ask why Christians personify abstraction, such as Word, Law, and Truth by Christ, when the Jews, who were the first Christians, did not. Again, the difference may have arisen because Roman numeral mathematics equates the abstract concept of number with its visible expression, indicating that is the way people thought in the Latin language. Roman numerals are merely drawings of the number of sticks required to represent the number. V is a drawing of four sticks with a slash to represent the fifth stick, converted to V for simplicity. Ten is a drawing of sticks with two slashes, converted to X for simplicity. The abacus and the counting board, which had very widespread use from ancient times to present, deal with the abstract concept of number as a visible entity: a bead or counter. Also, to those who use the abacus or counting boards as Romans did, the truths of mathematics are not separate from the user. For example, in Japan today, complex problems are worked by three or more abacus experts and majority rules as to what the right answer is. Objective proof is not attained. (Modern Roman Catholics use the principle of the abacus in the rosary.) Thus the mathematical knowledge of early Christian times could offer no objection to these Christian ideas.

When the Roman numeral user thought of three, he thought of this drawing of three sticks that is the Roman numeral. When he thought of other abstractions he thought of their visible expression. When he thought of law, he thought of the lawgiver. When he thought of justice, he thought of Justice, a blindfolded goddess holding scales. Liberty and Freedom are other goddesses; a statue of the first is in New York harbor and the other is on top the U.S. Capitol building in Washington, D.C.

This habit of personifying abstraction persists today, for example, in referring to the American cowboy, who "is the law" in some frontier town, referring to a policeman as the law, referring to the "long arm of the law," and referring to a book as the author, as equated with the author. Thus merely translating the Bible into Latin would cause these abstracts to be personified, because that is the way people thought in that language. In answer to the question, Christians personify abstraction because that was the thought system that informed most of those who became Christians. It is an expression of the ignorance of that day. However, personification of abstraction is and was alien to Judaism.

Let us consider what follows in the religious sphere from Law becoming a person. The Jew's relationship to his God is a legal relationship. If the Hebrew God and His Law become Persons of the Trinity, then man's relationship to that God becomes a relationship to a Person or Persons. The religious difference that follows, which we shall consider in this chapter, is that this relationship with its aspects tends to transcend all relationships to other persons, reaching its ultimate expression in the practice of celibacy. The practice of celibacy requires a banishment of thoughts of the opposite sex from one's mind. Thus the celibate is referred to as the "bride of Christ."

However, if the Hebrew God and His Law remain metaphysical and abstract, then this Law tends to transcend all other laws, religious and political. Thus Judaism has the potential of establishing constitutional government, rights and liberties, as

English-speaking peoples understand them, over what is now the entire Christian world.

As is well known, celibacy has been abandoned for some centuries in many Protestant denominations. However, the influence of the celibate mentality has anything but disappeared, as the following pages will show. By the celibate mentality is meant not the mind of the celibate of today, but more the thinking of celibates in medieval and later centuries. The celibates of this century are greatly influenced by universal public education, science, and technology.

Celibacy cannot ever be reconciled with Judaism. The first reason is an understanding attached to the Garden of Eden story that Eve is created because, "It is not good for man to be alone." (Jews as well as Christians are aware that the biblical origin of man lacks scientific validity. Jews recognize this story as an allegorical account of man's origin to which a moral lesson is attached.)

A second reason is that since Adam and Eve, having eaten of the tree of knowledge of good and evil, the Jewish understanding of such knowledge, which is knowledge of rule of Law, begins by opening one's eyes to the fact that girls are different from boys, by an awareness of sex and love and their implications. By an awareness that rule of law evolves out of what the weak consent to the strong. Thus "governments rule by consent of the governed," and strong-man rule is evil. The Christian understanding of this passage will be understood to be obviously that of a celibate clergy, which clergy have closed their eyes to this fact and implications. This clergy see this passage as Original Sin, requiring the descendants of Adam and Eve to be baptized.

A third reason is that a purpose of the Jewish rite of circumcision is to convey the understanding that sexual-mutilation, which celibacy is, is evil.

Thus, Jewish teachers and rulers have been men who experienced love between the sexes, eventually married, and raised families. Hence, Judaism is regarded as a family-type religion. And Judaism and Christianity differ to some extent as such love differs from celibate love for Christ.

The religions also differ because in Medieval Christianity the celibate understanding of the world was held as ideal and official, and the understanding of those who experience love between the sexes was held as inferior. This is one reason why Christianity is held to be an improvement on Judaism.

The idea of superiority of celibate love is a militaristic influence. Obviously he who loves God and country as much as the celibate loves Christ is generally a better soldier than he who is attached to a sweetheart or wife and family.

Some aspects of how love between the sexes differs from celibate love for Christ and how these aspects affect the religious differences are given below. It will be seen that the Hebrew understandings are the common sense ones on which common men who have experienced love between the sexes can agree. This agreement could form a basis for rule of common law, rule by common people in both the religious and political spheres and consequent overthrow of rule by a celibate clergy and militarists. It will be seen that the Christian meaning obscures such understandings and offers instead a sacrament or other concept that would tie the Christian to his authority and/or would withdraw or divide him from other men, that would divide and rule common men.

First, in love between the sexes, one's romantic fantasies are eventually tested against reality, because these fantasies are tied to a physically existing person whose behavior can be observed. On the contrary, the fantasies associated with love for Christ are never tested against reality because that Person is not present, or He is present only under the apppearance of bread and wine. He cannot be observed. Thus, the fantasies and love for Christ continue for centuries and Christians, celibate or otherwise, never do become aware of the extent to which they are dreaming, or that such fantasies constitute an emotional trap. For example, many engaged couples who look forward to a life of heavenly married bliss are eventually awakened by a rude shock. Christians look forward to a heaven hereafter and there is no rude shock to awaken them until after death. (Thus inherent in Judaism is the requirement that ideas, plans, and decisions must be grounded in reality, must be tested against reality.) The popular anti-Semitic idea that the Jews of the twentieth century could never be forgiven for what they did to Christ is an indication of how unaware Christians are that they are daydreaming.

Love between the sexes is tied to sex, which is undignified, but which is also a premium on pleasing others in this world. The celibate's lack of orientation to such undignified love, the lack of experience of the need to please others and of the humiliations that accompany such love and the lack of awareness that such fantasies by themselves tend to be wish fulfillment, leads him into the emotional trap of self-love, of seeing Christ as perfect and himself as approaching perfection through the imitation of Christ. He does not comprehend that no person is perfect. He is in the emotional trap of loving an idealization, a glorification of himself in which there is no basis for testing either party's perfection against reality. Thus, there is nothing to prevent the growth of conceit, self-righteousness, and a holier-than-thou attitude, or there is nothing to prevent the taking a stereotyped view of other people. Or the idea that one can speak for Christ, or be the Vicar of Christ, or know what Christ would have done, or know what would please Him. Or to prevent the idea that one can know Christ, who was a Jew, without knowing Judaism. Or to prevent the foolishness of dedicating one's entire life and the rights to one's body to Christ. These practices have caused divisions in Christian denominations because the attitudes are unrelated to reality and not sensible.

Love between the sexes carries with it a premium of accepting that which is unclean, unsanitary. In celibate love there is no such premium. Hence celibates and their followers have been intolerant of such as in their anti-Semitic remarks that you can even smell a Jew. This provided authorization for the Nazi "purges" and campaigns to "cleanse" Europe of Jews. This intolerance is reflected in the sacrament of Baptism: the sexual connotations of the Hebrew understanding are replaced by a sacrament that connotes a washing, cleansing action.

In the context of the Hebrew understanding of the Garden of Eden story, the celibates' position of approaching perfection through Christ, of imitating Christ, of being as God, cannot be valid because the serpent promises that if you eat, you shall be as gods. This they did and they sinned.

In comparison to celibate love, love between the sexes carries with it an awareness that the female figure and femininity are expressions of the similarity of every man's tender thoughts and desires and that such thoughts and desires can be the basis for unity among such men in the formation of a society in which gentlemen work out their differences without recourse to violence. Judaism provides genuine moral authorization for such a society. Christianity, on the other hand, seems to hold as ideal a unity in the violence of Christ's passion and death or a unity under Christ's authority.

In Judaism, knowledge of good and evil begins with an understanding that many aspects of femininity indicate that women are aware of men's thoughts and desires and are able to manipulate such for the purpose of leading men into the tender emotional trap of love, marriage, and family life, which effectively holds men down. They lead men into this trap by the seductive effect of sex as an expression of prestige, illusion, mystery, magic, glory, etc. In this trap a man is tied to blood relatives and attains prestige in the eyes of his wife and children.

Thus knowledge of good and evil begins with an awareness of the existence of emotional traps. From the Jewish standpoint, the Christian concept of God as a Person is an emotional trap, and celibacy a deeper, stronger trap. Just as the feminine figure and femininity lead millions of men into the tender trap, the same aspects of Christianity lead millions of men into this other trap. The central feature of this trap is that of a god-man, worthy of imitation by all men, placed on earth as a human sacrifice completely subject to His Father's will. By such He attains great good, honor, and glory in heaven forever as would those who would imitate Him. The authority's awareness of the thoughts and the desires of the Christian layman for prestige, illusion, magic, mystery, glory, etc., separate from sex and love, leads this layman into this trap, which is not tender, because it glorifies violence, torment, and death. The romantic daydreams of the celibate appear to the dreamer to have an eternally mysterious purpose and are intensely personal. Also Presences are felt which are attributed to supernatural beings.

In Judaism, knowledge of good and evil begins by realizing that if one simply follows one's emotions, one may find one's self under some female's thumb, as the celibate should find himself where he is, for the same reason, under the religious authority's thumb. And such knowledge begins by attaining an emotional independence from one's parents or any mother or father figure, or other charismatic leader. And an emotional independence from the brotherhood of the military which is the same as the brotherhood of the religious orders.

Thus, politics in Christian nations has been militaristic because young men are unaware of the emotional trap that is nationalism and martial spirit. And they do not recognize this Hebrew moral lesson as a basis for uniting against such militarists, because their view of it is obstructed by Original Sin and Baptism, which are alien to Judaism.

In the emotional trap that is the Christian religion, the Church, the Mystical Body, men are held down by authority but are tied to artificial blood relatives and attain prestige by being with Christ.

Love between the sexes is an expression of spontaneity, frivolity, and personal artistic taste, since the girl is a work of art. Thus such love cannot be expressed in organized controlled fashion. There never could be thousands or millions of men in love with the same woman. Celibate love carries with it no such understanding. Hence, millions of Christians are supposed to love Christ, providing authorization also for the silly adulation bestowed by millions on the celebrities of the day. Love between the sexes tends to encourage maturity and independence. Thus the couple are soon planning their own home independent of their parents' wishes. Again celibate love breeds no such traits. Instead the celibate life tends to be a drab, uniformed, regimented, monastic, overcontrolled, overorganized existence in which there is little individual expression because the celibates are living on daydreams. Thus to hold celibate love superior is to hold a uniformed, regimented, overcontrolled, overorganized community superior to that of a free society, thus authorizing again totalitarianism and militarism.

Love between the sexes, in being tied to sex, which always has a private aspect, conveys awareness of another's right of privacy, which must be respected to some extent even in marriage. And such love conveys awareness that the other person has inalienable rights which limit the use of his or her body by the other person. Thus knowledge of good and evil in Judaism begins with an awareness of such rights. And with an awareness that romantic daydreams, whether of the opposite sex or of a religious, political, or military nature, usually require for their implementation a violation of another's rights and liberties. Celibate love conveys no such understanding, therefore, the celibate life has become one without the right of privacy and one without such inalienable rights. It has become a barracks-like existence in which one must confess one's sins, one's innermost thoughts to one's superiors, and hear others' confessions. To be known as a celibate is to make a public announcement of a very private matter, as a small child might do. To be a religious superior is to have the vow of celibacy from subordinates. This is to have a control over another's mind and body that is not expected in love between the sexes. And thus he who would become a celibate would not be likely to be aware of his own rights. Leadership by such persons provides authorization in the political sphere for rule by persons not conscious of their own or others' rights to privacy or to their own bodies. It holds as ideal rule by those willing to mutilate themselves to prove their love, dedication, and devotion to the fatherland as religious prove the same to Holy Mother Church.

Most important is that in love between the sexes, one must take total responsibility for one's words and acts. Self-control at all times is essential. One should never speak without considering the reaction that might be provoked in one's sweetheart, spouse, children or relatives. In celibate love there is no counterpart, because the other Person, Christ, is not present in a way that His reaction can be observed. Thus, the celibate clergy for centuries preached on anti-Semitism that provoked its culmination in Hitler's gas ovens. That the militaristic themes of Christianity provide authorization for a militaristic society goes unnoticed by a celibate clergy who worship the Prince of Peace. To be a celibate is to be unaware that men have self-control, men can govern their sexual desires, that men can govern themselves.

Love between the sexes is expressed in tenderness, gentleness. He who experiences such love lives in a gentle, tender world. Celibate love has no such aspect. Celibates live in this barracks-like world with Christ whose passion and death are central themes. The first kind of love authorizes political rule by distinguished gentlemen, the second rule by force, guns, and violence.

Second, the celibate understanding of the Bible obstructs awareness that, in Judaism, knowledge of good and evil begins with an understanding of the proper way of relating to the weaker sex. One must, in Judaism, be aware of one's own weakness, one's own longing to be loved even though one has faults, which longing can be satisfied only by consent of the weak, never by an act of violence or a use of the weak for one's selfish purposes. Thus one must acquire that sensitivity and insight into one's own personality and that of others that characterizes the lady's man, the gentleman. One must recognize that the behavior of one's sweetheart, or one's wife and family is to a great extent a reaction to one's own behavior. One must observe their behavior and correct one's own in accord. Thus one must internalize a self-correcting mechanism. Feedback refers to the operation of self-correcting mechanisms. Such mechanisms have had some use over the centuries but the concept is one formulated in the twentieth century in referring to the widespread use of computers for this purpose.

The God of the Hebrews is understood by Hebrews to use this process of feedback. He creates Adam, observes that it is not good for man to be alone, and creates Eve. He observes the earthly situation and brings about its correction. The earthly situation is one that regularly needs correction, which is to say that it is not perfect and never will be perfect. In the Garden of

Eden, Adam and Eve find themselves naked and correct this condition by putting on clothes. Thus knowledge of good and evil begins with knowledge of feedback. Thus the Hebrew religion is centered on God's Law, to which individuals can appeal in order to correct societies.

Feedback in modern mechanical devices concerns "governors": parts inherent in a mechanical system of checks and balances, the purpose of which is to maintain equilibrium during operations, that is to keep motors from running too fast or too slow and to make the mechanism fail safe. The governor is an integral part of the mechanical devices of the Industrial evolution, which originated in England about 1760. From there it spread to New England and gave rise to the same concept of checks and balances in British and American law and politics.

A world that regularly needs correction and, therefore, must have self-correcting means provided to it, evolves into a world that was corrected with the Redemption, the coming of Christ in the minds of celibates, because they do not experience the feedback inherent in the boy-girl relationship. Hence since the Redemption, men approach perfection and a state of sanctifying grace through reception of the sacraments, by imitating Christ who is perfect, and by becoming members of Christ's Mystical Body. To suggest that He or His Mystical Body be corrected is to no longer accept Him as God.

To understand and to participate in a political system based on the consent of the governed requires that rulers have the above insight into the weak, who are the ruled, a dependence on them, and an awareness that one is not perfect—one always needs self-correction. Also it is required that men agree to be gentlemen. Thus under this form of government, to receive consent might require the president or prime minister to "woo the public, perhaps to buy off the legislature, or even to prostitute himself." This form of government requires that the individual citizen see himself as weak, as consenting or not consenting to be led by a strong man, the president. Being so weak he must unite with others in a political party, he must, as must a woman, attract attention to be effective. The president or prime minister must be a man who needs to be loved and admired by the weak, the public, a man who wants to please them. Thus whether a man or woman, one must have sufficient empathy with the opposite sex to see the president as a person to whom one is tied, the terms of which are a constitution and bill of rights, and with whom one will criticize and debate and perhaps poke fun at, in order to gain some influence.

Thus, the president should not rule without consent for the same reason one should not do something else without consent. Nor should he lead the public into a compromising position, nor threaten the citizen with force or violence. Thus knowledge of good and evil begins by an awareness that one simply cannot follow one's urges, one must, as did Adam and Eve, put on one's clothes. One must play the game according to the rules. One must recognize that one's needs, one's desires, one's problems must be worked out without violence.

To hold the above form of government as ideal requires that one hold love between the sexes as ideal, rather than celibate love, which conveys no such understanding. The celibate relates to Christ, who is not weak. He is all-powerful, as is the religious superior to whom the celibate owes vows of obedience. And the celibate satisfies his longing to be loved through Christ, not to others in the world. Thus the celibate does not become aware of the proper way of relating to the weak or that he is weak, because Christ is always there like a big brother. The celibate must be strong enough to be ready to die for his faith at all times. His world has no weak people in it, or should have none. His desires to be loved by the opposite sex must be suppressed by the will, providing authorization for the iron-will characteristic of totalitarians. Thus, the celibate sees himself as one with the All-Powerful.

He who relates to the weaker sex sees himself as already very strong and has no need to relate to the All-Powerful. The celibate because of his vows does not see the weak. His personality retains aspects of those who are unable to experience love between the sexes: children and homosexuals. He lacks insight into the personalities of others or sympathy for them. He sees the world to some extent as do little boys who play with guns. These little boys shoot and kill each other and a few minutes later rise from the dead to play another day—as Christ died and rose from the dead. As soldiers killed in war are believed to have their souls rejoined to their bodies on the Last Day, therefore, war is just a game.

This childish mentality requires a big man, a big brother and the celibate sees himself as subject to Holy Mother Church and as being a member of his fatherland. He serves God as a member of a religious fatherland. He serves God as a member of a religious community that excludes girls. The Gospels are seen to be a story of grown men, each of whom has an emotional involvement with Christ as boy scouts have with their scoutmaster.

Thus the celibate also lacks awareness that many are attracted to the religion by themes of violence, bloodshed, bullying, and emasculation. And he lacks insight into the motives of his religious authority, providing authorization for a similar lack in the mind of the common man in the political sphere. Thus while wars have grown bigger and worse decade by decade, Christ is still regarded the Prince of Peace.

The celibate world is a jungle in which each of us must be strong, each man an island to himself. In this world people are inflexible and have to be forced to do anything, threatened with hell-fire and damnation. Vows of obedience are required, and people must be yelled at because they are so insensitive (providing authorization for the crudeness of radio and television broadcasting). One must segregate one's self and one's fellow strong men because one does not need the weak, which is a meaning of celibacy. One needs a hierarchy so one can identify with those at the top, who are the strong, the privileged. This jungle aspect is unrelieved by tenderness because the celibate's daily existence is so unrelieved. The passionate assaults women make on a celibate are often extremely serious threats to his remaining in the state of grace. So he must be iron-willed and must identify with the strong because the weak and tender are so threatening. But the celibate by his presence provokes such assaults.

In love between the sexes, there is a premium on having a

flexible personality and on making adjustments, because the relationship is a dynamic one. In celibate love there is no similar premium so the approach to perfection is characterized by an approach to rigidity and an excessive demand that others make any adjustments.

In the political sphere violence or threat of violence is required, in the celibate view of a well-ordered community. As are oaths of obedience, such as those ordered by Hitler from his soldiers. Celibates see the message of the Gospels as being that the greatest good in history was accomplished through the violence of Christ's crucifixion. This authorizes a tolerance of violence on television, in movies, and in comic books for children, tolerance of a high crime rate, of a high rate of automobile accidents, and of a continuous threat of world war.

Romantic fantasies of the opposite sex are often expressions of a desire to use the other person for one's selfish purposes. Celibate fantasies follow a similar theme. The celibate's approach to perfection tends to be a process in which what is unacceptable in one's self is personified outside one's self, so that one may see one's self as perfect and strong, so that one may be Christlike. It is a world in which "others are guilty, I am not. These others are inflictions on the innocent and on scapegoats, I am not." As Christ, a scapegoat, died for our sins. Thus the Jews are seen as having crucified Christ. Thus one is guilty by the sin of Adam until baptized. Thus the Devil is the source of evil. Thus the Jews of the Old Testament are regarded as ideals of holiness throughout the Christian world, but the Jews of today are despised. Thus those approaching perfection tend to blame subordinates for their own mistakes. These attitudes evolve out of the celibate condition. Those who view themselves in a boy-girl relationship know that rarely is one party guilty and not the other, because each is reacting so dynamically to the other. One accepts one's self as imperfect because the other person does.

The celibate satisfies his longing to be loved through relating to Christ rather than to people in this world. Therefore, he does not need these people except to use them in his romantic mythical world, to personify that which is unacceptable in himself, and to bully them. He tends to bully people and to be impressed by bullying because he is prevented from proving his manhood in the accepted sense by his vow. The vow of obedience subjects the cleric to an unlimited amount of bullying by superiors. Christ was bullied to death by Roman soldiers. In imitating Him, one would subject one's self to bullying. Celibacy itself is a form of bullying. The goal in this world of bullying is to get on top or to identify with those on top so as to bully everyone else, to emasculate everyone else (by vows of celibacy and other restrictions on sex and love), to provoke the weak to violence so that the weak can be beaten, for the fun of seeing them beaten and tormented. This personal need on the part of Christian authority explains many aspects of the Christian departure from Judaism. The Infinite becomes limited because the bully needs a Big Man. Law becomes a Person so that the ordinary man is stripped of any standing before authority. Hence he can be bullied. The concept of the Mystical Body is invented so that the ordinary man is reduced to simply a part, an arm, an instrument, a means by which others can be bullied. One should believe in the forgiveness of sins, the resurrection of the body, and life everlasting because these assist one in being a soldier, in being cannon fodder, in being a means of bullying others.

This also explains the popularity of the bullfight in many Christian nations. A dumb animal that is a symbol of masculinity is led into an arena and attracted by shiny capes. It is continually provoked to attack so it can be spectacularly emasculated, so that people can have the fun of seeing it beaten and tormented. By this bullying and emasculation, the matador gains prestige as a symbol of masculinity, just as the religious authority gains status because he emasculates subordinates, and the political authority gains status by emasculating the enemy in war.

The Christian authority has taken the Jews' Bible and appended to it a Testament that authorizes a contradictory meaning of the text, which meaning proves to the Christian that the Jew is wrong when he was once right. The meaning has the purpose of provoking the Jew to attack and, because everyone knew that the Jews were limited in number and weak, the Jew would be spectacularly beaten, emasculated. By such, the Christian authority gains prestige in his mythological view of himself as a Vicar of Christ, because he is unaware that the weak are not to be bullied. However, because the Jew was provoked to attack, Christians found the Jew a threat and therefore needed a militaristic authoritarianism to keep those who threaten in their place. Hence the Jews had to be herded into ghettos and finally exterminated.

In Judaism, knowledge of good and evil begins with putting on one's clothes, in resisting any provocation to bully the other person to prove one's status or manhood, and in resisting any provocation to be used for this purpose. Thus such knowledge conveys the lesson that provocation is an emotional trap, as the bull is caught by the matador in an emotional trap.

Love between the sexes conveys the lesson that one can never adopt that principle of the Roman orgy, "grab whatever you want," because what one wants belongs to another. Because the celibate and his followers have not learned this lesson, they see nothing amiss about a religion built on concepts grabbed from the Hebrew Bible and used to provide status.

Thus, in Judaism knowledge of good and evil begins with recognizing that there is a stronger and a weaker sex, with the development of empathy with the opposite sex, with the ability to see one's self as strong in relationship to one's family, and with the ability to see one's self as weak with relationship to rulers. Knowledge begins with recognizing that the first function of Law is to prevent the weak, however defined, from being bullied to death—as the soldier is bullied by his general and by the enemy.

Third, celibate love for Christ has obstructed awareness that in Judaism, knowledge of good and evil begins with awareness that one relates to the weak mainly on terms set by the weak. One must enter into partnership, play the game according to the rules, give and take, and compromise with them. Basic to such awareness must be a recognition that the weak, whether women or children, or men with respect to political authority, are rational sensible creatures. The terms of the relationship will arise out of this rationality. In love between the sexes there is great premium on comprehending this rationality.

In celibate love for Christ there is no comparable lesson or premium. The primary relationship is to a mythical figure who is believed, who is not reasoned with, and there is, therefore, no premium on dealing with that Person or His terms. He is not present to state His terms. This Figure is all-powerful. Hence, in the celibate world, there are or should be no weak and no limit on bullying. There is no consciousness of terms or compromises or playing ball and hence there are no rules and no laws separate from rulers. Hence celibates often see the dealing with the other person on his or her terms that is characteristic of relationships with the opposite sex and of parliamentary democracy as indications of spinelessness, a lack of masculinity (!), in comparison to the moral rigidity of celibates. Because the celibate personality has developed no faculty for partnership or reasoning with the opposite sex, he knows only two alternatives: to dominate (bully) his fellow beings or to withdraw from them. Thus vows of obedience are required from candidates to the religious life. The Christian religion is highly authoritarian, and it provides a mythology into which to withdraw for identification with an all-powerful godlike Person. The mythology provides a basis, a big brother by which the celibate can control his fellow man. And it provides a Mystical Body, which is the subject of another chapter, by which Christians can become one body and blood with Christ.

Thus, celibate love obstructs awareness that in Judaism knowledge of good and evil begins also by accepting the standdard of behavior of the gentleman: one who submits to one's peers and the opposite sex as the final criterion of the rightness and wrongness of his acts, which submittal requires one to accept the basic rationality of others. This is in comparison to the celibate's submittal only to Christ as the final criterion, the agent's submittal to only a dictator, or the child who submits only to his mother. (Thus the celibate sees the ideal marriage, that between Mary and Joseph, as celibate. Neither party submits to the other—ever.)

Also, the celibate must not enter the marketplace, because to do such is to submit to the customer as a criterion of correctness ("the customer is always right"). Hence the deprecation of financial success in Christianity, the vows of poverty in some religious orders, and Christ's call to leave the marketplace.

This submittal to others as the final criterion is basic to acceptance of rule of common law as Jews, Englishmen, and Americans understand it: law as the expression of the consensus of what is right and wrong. Submittal to one's peers, as in trial by jury, begins with a man submitting to the opposite sex as the final criterion. Because the celibate has closed his eyes to the fact that girls are different from boys, he has not acquired such sensitivity or insight and he does not submit to his peers, his equals. Nor does he want anything from his fellow men, thus, he has taken vows of poverty, chastity, and obedience. He is isolated in Christ. Therefore he does not need to work out anything with his fellowman as an equal. And therefore he needs to refer to no consensus of what is right and wrong. He is the authority because he is so close to Christ. His only way of relating to others is if they are also with Christ. Hence in his mind the consensus of what is right and wrong becomes Christ. The terms on which men agree become Christ. In this mind, the terms on which men agree become the dictates of the Top Man on whom all agree. And thus, rule of law (Law) as Jews, Englishmen and Americans understand it, evolves into the Roman Canon law and the Continental Civil law. But this evolution takes place only in the celibate mind, because this mind does not comprehend the opposite sex as rational and, therefore, such a mind does not comprehend law (Law) as an expression of the consensus of rationality. Hence popes have regularly set aside consitutional government on the continent during the last two centuries. Hence the celibate clergy never understood Judaism as a rational system, but only as a curse.

The above is not to say that celibates and their followers isolated in Christ are ignorant of law or misunderstand law, or violate law. It is to say that the isolate finds law incomprehensible, because in the isolate's thoughts the weaker sex are not there to be related to with terms. He does not see girls as different from boys. The weaker sex are not weak, they are threatening to celibates because they threaten their state of grace. There are only the strong, those who should be strong, and those who threaten the strong. Thus one must recognize that awareness of law (Law) begins with an awareness of desire for the opposite sex and the necessity to limit action on such desire.

Thus in Judaism, knowledge of good and evil also begins by recognizing that such knowledge has many layers and aspects of meaning which must be interpreted with great sensitivity, as are the words spoken in tender relationships. He who is isolated in Christ has closed his eyes to this. He can see only his own meaning of the Bible.

Such knowledge also begins by recognizing the premium that is on actually understanding others and working things out with others. From this it would follow that dissatisfaction with rule of law (Law) may go hand in hand with a dissatisfaction with the opposite sex. To return to our earlier question as to why celibacy cannot ever be reconciled with Judaism, a fourth reason is that the sin of the Snake in the Garden of Eden is seduction of the innocent. The Snake is a phallic symbol and he promises, "You shall be as gods." Celibacy keeps the man innocent so he can be seduced by the imitation of Christ. Again, knowledge of good and evil begins with men learning the common sense advice given girls in their relationship with boys and the political implications of such advice. With an awareness that seducers promise "pie in the sky" and the seduced tend to believe such promises. With an awareness that "all the stories told by the strong to the weak have one ending: the use of the weak by the strong." With an awareness that the strong try to catch the weak in an emotional trap and the weak tend to enjoy being caught. With an awareness that one wants to believe one's romantic daydreams, wants others to believe them, and is intolerant of those who do not believe them. As the celibate clergy and their followers have for centuries wanted all to believe in Christ and have been intolerant of nonbelievers, such as Jews.

Also, knowledge of good and evil begins by the stronger sex

accepting the talkativeness of the weaker sex—by political leaders accepting the talkativeness of the ordinary citizen, by acceptance of the right of free speech and free assembly, and in modern times, freedom of the press.

Let us consider Christian beliefs in the light of this clarification.

1.   Before Christ, these are the alternative Christian beliefs:

a) The Hebrew religion was valid.

This means that knowledge of good and evil began with learning the self-evident truths implied in the observation that "girls are different from boys." God was recognized as not a person by the Graven Image Commandment.

b) The Hebrew religion was valid but Christian belief was valid also.

This means it was right to understand and accept the Hebrew Law based on the self-evident truths implied in that "girls are different from boys," and it was right also to close one's eyes to such, to see this Law as the Person of Christ, to enter the emotional trap created by this understanding, and to accept rule by a celibate clergy. These ideas were right also but they simply had not yet been revealed to be true. This position is untenable because it requires contradictory propositions to be true at the same time. This Christian position ignores the Graven Image Commandment, it ignores that God as a Person was characteristic of the idol worship of the peoples around the Jews, and it ignores the vast behavioral differences that follow from the idea that God is a Person. Such as that this concept is a means of controlling people.

2.   At some time during Christ's life, the Christian religion became valid and is valid today. At this time the self-evident truths of the proper way of relating to the weak were set aside. One no longer needed to rule by consent of the weak. Henceforth an authoritarian celibate clergy would rule and men would

be divided into those still having inherited Original Sin and those baptized. Also at this time, the God of the Hebrews became a Person.

Obviously, the self-evident truths referred to above have not and cannot be set aside. What actually happened is that the Hebrew understanding was abandoned in favor of a militaristic understanding because people and authorities thought they needed men who were not concerned with a sweetheart back home, men who were strong, iron-willed soldiers. This militaristic understanding and leadership, "rule by the strong," has remained deeply entrenched for centuries. Thus the Gospels contain Hebrew themes on which the Christian militaristic understanding has been forced. Christ is worshipping the God of the Hebrews who is not a person, but on the contrary, He is also completely subject to that God as a Person and His personal relationship to that God transcends all other personal relationships.

This supposed evolution of God into a Person raises the question as to why this evolution would take place. It is clear that this evolution took place because that is one aspect of the fantasies needed by celibates who are already isolated from anyone in this world. But in the minds of those who relate on an adult level to the opposite sex, the truths of Judaism that follow from "girls are different from boys" are as true as they ever were, because these truths are self-evident. There is no reason to think that such truths have evolved in Original Sin and Baptism. The idea is absurd.

Secondly, this evolution took place because that is the fantasy needed by those who claim to be morally superior, to be moral authorities, to be approaching perfection, and to whom sex and rule of law are undignified. In other words this is the fantasy needed by a celibate clergy to keep itself on top, to control the weak by other than consent. The millions of common people who do not need such fantasies do not need to believe that this evolution took place. The evolution requires that a God whose first moral lesson that girls are different from boys, become a God who holds it ideal for men to be emasculated and women be defeminized in the religious life and that girls be viewed as no different from boys, that is, as children view one another, as brothers view sisters, as children view father and mother. Hence the names for such religious.

3.   After Christ, these are the alternative Christian beliefs:

a) The Hebrew religion is still valid but obsolete or inferior.

The previous pages have shown that there is nothing obsolete about the Hebrew understanding of this aspect of their religion. Girls are as different from boys as they ever were. To say that the Hebrew understanding is inferior is to say that celibate love for Christ and the love Christ had for his fellow man are superior to that between the sexes. This is a central Christian theme. This theme obstructs awareness of the important personality differences that follow from primarily relating to the opposite sex, compared to he who relates only to Christ. Secondly, it obstructs awareness of how one should relate to the weak. One must obtain the consent of the weak. In Judaism this lesson has great religious significance and it provides genuine moral authorization for the proposition that "governments rule by consent of the governed." The Christian theme would hold this proposition obsolete or inferior to the idea that governments rule (as does the Heirarchy) without anyone's consent.

This belief would again hold it right and also wrong in the same instant to relate to a graven image of God, an obviously impossible position.

b) The Hebrew religion is no longer valid.

One wonders how these self-evident truths of Judaism could be no longer valid when they are obviously valid to all but celibates and their followers. The Christian belief must be simply a means of preventing common people from uniting on these truths for the purpose of ridiculing and then deposing a celibate clergy that thinks it has a right to rule without consent. And eventually deposing a political leadership that thinks it has moral authorization to the same right. For the self-evident truths that follow from "girls are different from boys" to be no longer valid requires that everyone have become a homosexual. It requires that men be emasculated and women be defeminized as in the religious life. This actually is a celibate ideal of the world. The celibate must see girls as no different from boys. Because such persons were for centuries the only ones in many communities who were literate, educated, had status, money, leisure time, etc., millions followed their leadership without question.

Politics has to do with the power to use force. This religious difference has much to say about how force shall be used.

The idea that the law is a person authorizes an orientation to the dictates of the top man, to the established authority, rather than to constitutional government. To hold Christianity superior to Judaism holds such one man rule superior to rule of Law (law). It is to hold as ideal a relationship to the strong, to He who is all powerful, rather than relationship to the weak. It is to authorize the citizen to view himself simply as an agent of the top man, the strong man, to see himself as one with the strong, never as weak as giving consent or not giving consent to be ruled. Hence, Christianity provides authorization for a militaristic hierarchical society.

The vow of celibacy is an expression of willingness to live out one's life as if one had been mutilated sexually by one's superiors. Holding this life as ideal holds as ideal a military career and a willingness to be led into battle for mutilation and death by one's superiors.

Rule by a celibate clergy authorizes political rule by persons with the same views as celibates and imitative behavior by the man in the street. Let us consider these views and their political authorization. These will be seen to be more dilemmas on which Christians in totalitarian nations are impaled.

Firstly, a political leader who embraces a fantasy life, who fails to confront the workaday problems of earning a living, who is regarded as the perfect charismatic leader and who dreams of attaining a "Lebensraum" or "Worker's Paradise" is authorized. Whether the fantasies make practical sense or not is irrelevant to him and his followers. In this movement, men become emotionally involved with the Fuehrer, his goals, and the Fatherland.

This leader manipulates the men under him by the award of medals for bravery in battle, etc. From an oath of obedience to him the only outlet is death. Invasions of privacy under such governments are common.

Secondly, a political leader who is unaware of his faults, who is self-righteous, and holier-than-thou is authorized. For these reasons such a leader would not accept international law or would deal as an equal with foreign leaders.

Thirdly, a rigid, iron-willed personality is held as ideal. This is expressed in such as Stalin's name, which means steel, in Bismarck, the Iron Chancellor, in the Iron Cross military awards, and in Peter, which means rock. Such a personality is of obvious military value.

Fourthly, in such a society the citizen should not see himself as weak. He should see himself as does the celibate: as being one with the strong, the all-powerful, in this case the state, which is conceived as a person and the citizen as a member of the body politic, as Christians are members of the Mystical Body. The political leader and the citizen should view the world as a jungle in which we, the nation, must be strong, because other nations threaten. Therefore we shall threaten them. This is a thoroughly familiar picture to students of modern European history. Other nations and their soldiers commit atrocities, we do not. Because the world is a jungle and is so threatening, we need a strong man who must be given a free hand to rule. Everyone needs to feel the presence of this strong man because the world is so threatening. Thus one should say, "Heil Hitler," on greeting another. Even a telephone call could not be made in Nazi Germany without feeling Hitler's presence, as Christians feel Christ's presence for the same reason. And Hitler's government also exterminated the weak, the unfit, the inferior. (This jungle aspect of the religion apparently provided authorization for the Social Darwinism of the last century: the survival of the fittest in the economic sphere.)

Thus one should see one's self as one with the strong, in one army with the strong for the purpose of provoking and bullying the weak. As the celibate has a mythology that authorizes him to dominate others, a political leader urges his people to recognize themselves as having the status provided by the ancient Teutonic mythology and Christianity, to see themselves as a master race, threatened by the Jews.

In imitation of the celibate who has a mythology that authorizes him to dominate and provoke others, some white Americans see themselves as having the status provided by Christ who was a white man. Since men are made to God's Image, the nonwhite races are subhuman, apelike, and threatening. Thus, a black man is referred to as a bogeyman, a spook. Some Americans see the mythology of the personification of the United States by Uncle Sam as an indication that this is a white man's country. Thus nonwhites, because they threaten, may be herded into reservations as Japanese-Americans were in California in World War II.

The conspicuous consumption of material goods seems to carry with it a mythology that authorizes he who consumes to dominate those on a lower standard of living, to consider himself better than they, and to provoke them to jealousy. Those on top are seen by those lower to use their time, money, and power not to help the common man get out from under, but to hold him down. And to provoke him. Such feelings lie waiting for a dictator to channel such rage against a target.

The celibate's attitude toward terms and conditions of relationships among humans is of enormous importance in politics. The idea that all relationships have rules, that one should play the game according to the rules and that one should be a good loser is basic to Hebrew Law as well as British and American law and is reflected in the great interest in sports in these nations. The celibate attitude is that there are no rules, one simply relates to He who is all-powerful. If one can dominate one's fellow man one does, if not, one withdraws into the daydream. One never meets one's fellowman as an equal. The celibate position is to a great extent that of a sore loser. He has read the Jewish Bible and finds that he, not being a Jew, is ignored; he is a loser. But this is a meaning he has forced on the text. He does not see that anyone can become a Jew and that all should. Since he has lost this Old Testament game, there must be something wrong with the rules. Hence, the rules become an all-powerful Person to whom he relates. Through the Mystical Body he can become a part of that Person. Then he can become the rules. Thus he plays the game as a winner because he is the rules. Hence the innumerable denominations in Christianity, none of which seem to be able to play ball with any of the others.

The sore-loser mentality pervades the religion because all that can be won through the religious life is the power to dominate others, and this is attained only by losing through vows one's right to independence, privacy, sex, and so on, in sum everything else. Again the celibate world is a jungle composed of men who seek only power to dominate others, providing authorization for similar militaristic behavior of leaders in the political sphere. All this is in imitation of Christ who won power, redemption through torment and death. This mentality is related to and authorizes militarism in which one wins great honor and glory through mutilation or death in battle. The more one is willing to be tormented, the more one wins. The more one loses, the more one wins. Everyone wins by losing except the top man who wins by using losers—because in the military there are winners and there are the dead. There are no good losers because militarism is without rules.

Because Christians have so completely ignored Judaism, they are unaware of their predicament of having made a departure to a religion that authorizes this militaristic personality type and holds it ideal.

Thus this aspect of the Christian irreconcilability with Judaism is in no sense a mystery. The Christian understanding is simply an expression of the militarism and romanticism of Roman times that ignores the Jewish understanding.

So we have another reason why Jews world-wide are in agreement on the essentials of their religion. This essential is common sense learned from the universal experience of love between the sexes. And we have another reason why Christians will never agree on the essentials of their religion: there can be no consensus except by force in a thought system in which the common sense learned from this experience does not apply.

Thus Jews and Christians read the same Bible and each derive a different meaning from it because the Christian reads it as does the celibate, in an insensitive fashion, and therefore, misses the Hebrew meaning.

Four

Abstraction: Law Becomes a Person Who Sets Aside the Law

Another aspect of the religious difference that follows from Law becoming a Person is that in Judaism the Law cannot be set aside. In Christianity Christ as this Law sets it aside and institutes personal rule.

This law (Law) in Judaism, in British and American law, and in modern mathematics and science is supreme. It is based on self-evident truths and forms one rational system which rules all entities. No man can set it aside, though an antiquated understanding can be set aside. Thus all men are equal before it. In Christianity this law (Law) becomes Christ who is supreme. He rules all entities. He sets aside the Hebrew Law as popes set aside the constitutional law in many European nations. Christ also set aside the laws of science by the miracles He worked and He has set aside the laws of mathematics by limiting infinity.

Thus Christians conceive Jesus of Nazareth, King of the Jews, in a different world from Kings David and Solomon of the Jews. They were ruled by the Law and were equal to all other men. Christ is and was this Law. He was not created equal to all other men, nor are all men equal before Christ as all men are equal before the Law.

By the miracles Christ worked, He proves His divinity and the validity of His teachings to Christians. Judaism does not depend on miracles for its validity to Jews. Its Law is accepted because it is a statement of self-evident truths in agreement with scientific truths. The miracles in the Hebrew Bible are recognized by Jews as stories added years after the event. Miracles are not worked by the God of the Hebrews because such are violations of His Law expressed as scientific laws: the Law that governs all entities.

Having defined this religious difference that has a mathematical expression, we should ask why Christians personify laws that rule all entities: the Hebrew Law, constitutional law, and the laws of mathematics and science. Secondly, we should ask why Christians believe this Person set aside these laws (Laws). The Hebrew conception of these laws (Laws) is very ancient. The concept underlies the laws of addition, subtraction, multiplication, and division, which were known before 3000 B.C. In Euclidean geometry, compiled about 323 B.C., one law also rules all entities. The geometry is one rational system based on a few axioms and postulates which are of the nature of self-evident truths. The alphabet, as compared with picture writing, is one rational system ruling all written communications (but not based on self-evident truths). Each letter is articulated with a specific sound. Picture or character writing, as it exists in the Orient today, is, on the contrary, an assemblage of separate writing inventions, each with its own rules.

The Christian personification of these laws (Laws) is from old Greek and Roman religious and legal ideas. In these religions, one god-man rules all gods and men. The Roman emperors were the law, were deified, and ruled the Roman world. Roman law was an assemblage of edicts by magistrates who were appointed by the emperor. In doubtful cases the emperors's decision was requested, whose rulings always had the force of law. The courts were agencies of the ruling authorities who made the law, they were not ruled by law. From time to time, these edicts would be revised and settled because some emperors had set aside the laws of others and there were many contradictions. This law was simply administrative law, law by which the top man gets things done. Before this law all men were not created equal because none were equal to the emperor. Nor was there much of an attempt to base this law on self-evident truths.

The Roman pontiffs have ruled their Church with the same legal system, called Roman Canon law. There have been innumerable contradictions in it over the centuries, which are resolved by appeal to the new pontiff who may set aside the old law, as the Vatican II Ecumenical Council is well known for having done. In nations whose citizens are knowledgeable in the laws of constitutional government, mathematics, science, and technology, this Council's decisions have created widespread disbelief, because it showed Church law as simply personal opinion of the top man.

Basic to the Roman and Christian thought system is the observation that all men are not created equal in any visible way. Hence a man can be a god. Roman society at the time of Christ was in harmony with this understanding. Slaves at the bottom of the Roman world were nothing. Their lives could be expended at will for the entertainment of crowds in the Colosseum. Nor did all free men have equal standing, because some men were given privileges by the Roman rulers for military services.

It is clear from the above that Christians personify the Hebrew Law and believe that it can be set aside because they are totally unaware that they are doing such. The Christian understanding of law is that of the Romans and is unrelated to the Hebrew.

It was said previously that the modern understanding of the political aspects of the Hebrew Law is British and American law. The modern understanding of the political aspects of the Roman Canon law is the Continental Civil law. This latter is law based on guidelines set up by the lawmaking authority: the monarchy, nobility, parliament, or dictator, as the Code Napoleon. The nation's judiciary is thus bound by a code of the nation's sovereign. There has historically been no right of appeal to self-evident truths under this law because there has been no awareness of such law to which to appeal over the sovereign's head. Thus the executive and judicial branches of this form of rule are merged. To distinguish it from this law, British and American law as well as the Hebrew Law is called Common law, because it is law built by the common people.

Having defined this religious difference that has a mathematical expression, let us consider what differences follow in the religious sphere. This Law is based on truths acceptable to all

men as self-evident. These truths in Judaism provide the fundamentals on which the Jew enters into dialogue with God and on
which he can enter into dialogue with his fellow Jews, with
members of his family, and Jewish religious and political authorities. Secondly, these truths over the centuries have provided a
basis for such as ordinary Jews, Englishmen, and Americans to
unite for the purpose of limiting the power of authorities, religious and political. These truths become in Christianity, Christ,
who is Truth, as in His words, "I am the Way, the Truth and
the Life."

Truths acceptable to all men as self-evident become Christ
who is Truth but not in a self-evident objective sense. He
becomes Truth in a personal, emotional and mythical sense.
"Believe in the Lord Jesus Christ and you will be saved" implies
that unless one accepts Christ as Truth, one will not be saved.
On the contrary, one accepts the self-evident truths of mathematics, of the Hebrew Law, and the Constitution not because
one will be saved if one does, but because one has studied them
until he understands them as truths. Thus the relevant effect of
Christian belief is to create a thought system in which the self-
evident truths that could be a basis for settling differences among
common men are replaced by beliefs of personal emotional
meaning—a thought system in which an authority is required to
settle differences, and in which men will always be divided as to
which authority they will accept. For example the millions of
English-speaking peoples who are able to unite on the politically
relevant self-evident truths of the Hebrew Laws are divided into
innumerable Christian denominations because they are unable
to unite on Christ as Truth. Christ as Truth provides a basis for
unity of ordinary people only if they can agree on a common
authority. Thus German Catholics and Lutherans could not
unite in opposition to Hitler. They had no common authority
other than Hitler.

Hebrew self-evident truths provide a basis for unity of
common people but Christ as Truth does not. Therefore, in
Christianity, unity has historically been provided by an authority
and by a common enemy, usually the Jews (this is also a familiar

technique of totalitarian rulers), a we versus they view of the world. Thus the basis on which ordinary Jews could unite for the purpose of limiting the power of religious authorities becomes Christ, or the Vicar of Christ, or the "Christ among us" as some Protestant ministers are called.

Men who accept the Hebrew Law, which is based on self-evident truths, can govern themselves in the religious and political spheres. If one believes that this Law can become a Person, as is fundamental to Christianity, then one is in effect believing that men do not and should not govern themselves.

Because, first, this is to believe that any basis for dialogue or consensus, which the Hebrew Law is, can be set aside or can become a person. This Christian belief is an expression of the absolutism of the established Roman rulers at the time of Christ. It is an expression that the only consensus among all subjects of these rulers was acceptance of their rule. And it is an expression of the romanticism and the hero-worship of Roman times and of celibate love of Christ that agreement on such love sets aside and is superior to any dialogue, consensus or agreement between husband and wife. It is an expression of rule by any established government or established church. That such is established means that it is not subject to consent or lack of consent to be governed and that dialogue and consensus can be set aside. Thus the belief that the Word was made Flesh has the effect of stripping the common man of any basis for unity in opposing religious or political authorities.

Because second, this leaves the only basis for agreement in the religious and political spheres to be the authorities themselves or mythical persons. Since the authorities can set aside any basis for dialogue and they control the mythology, one must follow them blindly or one is out. In the religious sphere, this has meant to accept Papal rule or to become a Protestant against such. In the political sphere, this means accepting an autocratic regime or being herded into ghettos or concentration camps.

Thus, if the Word was made Flesh, the authority has become the indispensable man. To dispense with him would dispense with he who resolves disagreements and is a unifying force, who is the prince or pope of peace. This would lead to the chaos which we have seen in the Christian world since the Protestant revolt. The authority is therefore justified in doing whatever is necessary to maintain himself in power. To reduce the number of disagreements brought before him, he is justified in telling people what to say, think, and read: to censor, and to hold them guilty until proved innocent. No one should mention his doubts about the authority and woe betide he who would turn away from him. The authority can have no loyal opposition because such would be disruptive. Other violations of inalienable rights may be required. A nation dedicated on the proposition that all men are created equal is seen as unworkable because such a proposition leaves no room for the authority, who must be unequal—superior to other men. A constitution to limit his powers in order to protect peoples' rights is understood to limit the authoritiy's power to settle disagreements, his power to prevent chaos. This has been the conduct of the Papacy through the centuries. As long as people accepted it as the leader of all Christians, it could settle disagreements among Christian nations and be a limit on the tyranny of political leaders. When the Roman Church broke into churches, people were left with no substitute but violence, war, and revolution. In this thought system the very word "freedom" is synonymous with disorder.

Because third, if these truths can be set aside, one is left with no means of proving he is right except by being willing to fight, to be mutilated, or to die for what one believes in just as Christ was willing to undergo scourging at the pillar, crucifixion and death to prove he is the Son of God. Thus Christ's passion and the torments of martyrs have historically been Christian themes of great importance. From this it follows that he who would enter the religious life must prove his faith by being a celibate, that is, by living out his life as if he had been sexually mutilated. Service in the military and heroism on the battlefield are proofs of patriotism.

Thus a peaceful society, in which men can settle their

disputes in courts of Law, namely the Jewish biblical world, is replaced by a militaristic one: by the Church upon Earth, the Church Militant. Thus life under Christ is necessarily a struggle, as is the fight against temptation, the world is a jungle, and this is an improvement. This conception of the world has great appeal, as witness the innumerable wars in the Christian nations and the appeal of a book entitled *My Struggle*.

Judaism, on the contrary, requires that each young man demonstrate a correct understanding of the Law from its origin in biblical times to the present day, as a means of settling disagreements with one's fellowman and with authorities, as a basis of opposing authorities, and as a means of proving one's self right. Christianity, in being a departure from Judaism, does not urge its adherents to acquire a rigorously correct understanding of a legal text, code, or document, which understanding is a responsibility of citizenship in a democratic society.

Instead Christianity provides authorization for the principle of a German democracy: the leader is elected, but then enjoys unconditional authority, subject to no rule of law, as Hitler was elected, and as men choose to follow Christ. Again, this is the dilemma on which Christians under Hitler were impaled.

Christ, having set aside self-evident truths of the Hebrew Law, constitutional law and the laws of science and mathematics, would appear to authorize an educational system based on something other than common sense dialogue and ability acquired through learning. Central to historical Christianity is the idea of ability conferred by Christ the King. For example, in the Gospels, the Apostles have knowledge of marketable skills but are understood to be nothing without Christ. With Christ they became great preachers. With the sacraments, especially Confirmation and Holy Orders they bcame able to confer abilities to be soldiers of Christ and to discharge the powers of the priesthood. This Christian idea necessarily replaces the common sense Hebrew emphasis on learning the Law and on acquiring ability through study and practice.

In the political sphere, these Christian beliefs provided authorization for a king who conferred abilities as a political and/or military leader—creating dukes, earls, knights, and barons—just as popes created pastors, bishops and cardinals. Much of the blame for the mass slaughter of World War I was placed on those on whom abilities had been conferred. Thus the overthrow of the nobility or at least a withdrawal of their privileges followed this war.

Christians—in holding that the Hebrew religion was valid until Christ's time and since then Christianity is valid, and also that the Hebrew religion is valid, or invalid—are saying what in terms of these mathematically expressible concepts?

1. Before Christ, these are the alternative Christian beliefs:

a) The Hebrew religion was valid. Then, as today, Jews worshipped the God of the Hebrews and reverenced His Word. Jews have never worshipped His Word, because God's Word is not God. The written Word is kept in a tabernacle in the temple. His Covenant with Noah was, and is, understood to rule all men, and before it all men are equal. This Christian belief says that before Christ, the propositions on which British and American law are based were valid.

b) The Hebrew religion was valid, but the Word was with God as the Second Person of the Trinity, because Christ had not yet been born. This belief ignores the biblical accounts that Jews had the Word of God before Christ and it was not a Person. Part of it was written about twenty-six hundred years ago, a person cannot be written. And this belief ignores that the Jews' Bible is an account of how ordinary Jews, in dialogue with God, their leaders and their fellow Jews developed their concepts of rule of Law out of the consensus over the centuries. Instead the Christian belief is that this lawmaking function was centered in one Man, the Word who was made Flesh. This is obviously erroneous. The Christian belief completely ignores the Hebrew understanding. Secondly, the Christian says that the self-evident truths of the Hebrew Laws were truths and they were Christ who is Truth at the same time: truth was abstract and a Person at the same time, but that Person had not yet been born. This cannot be anything but nonsense. Thus the Christian belief dismisses the Hebrew Law as arbitrary, basically silly practices and ideas, which belief is still very widely held.

2. At some time during Christ's life, the Christian religion became valid and is valid today. At that time the Word became Flesh. This is no reason to worship the Word—assuming It could become Flesh because Jews never worshipped the Word, so why should Christians? Secondly, it is difficult to understand how the Law, of which British and American law is a part, can become a Person Who should be received under the appearance of bread and wine. Jews, Englishmen and Americans know that this makes no sense. The belief "the Word was made Flesh and dwelt among us" cannot be anything but a lie. It is about as sensible as saying that, if the Statue of Liberty and the Statue of Freedom could be broken into enough pieces, each American could be given his liberty and freedom and we would have no further use for the Constitution and our courts of law. If enough pieces of this steel and concrete could be produced, freedom and liberty could be spread around the world, as the Roman Church has spread the Word of God around the world as a piece of bread.

Thirdly, the fact that the Word and its self-evident truths are still in the Bible, where anyone can find it, indicates that it has not become a person. It remains an abstraction. It would appear that this Christian idea developed in an age which did not even imagine the invention of printing or universal public education.

Fourthly, this raises the question as to why the Hebrew Law became flesh and the laws of mathematics and science, which are part of this Law, remains as abstract as ever. It is clear that to Christians the Word was made Flesh only in a daydream sense. Christ working miracles sets aside these laws, but His miracles do not make these laws become flesh.

If the Word became Flesh at Christ's birth, or at any subsequent time in His life, then Christ's study of the Word in the temple as a Child and His practice of the Hebrew religion until

His crucifixion, is nonsense, because He is what He is studying and practicing. If Christ actually did set aside the Law, why does the Gospel quote Him as saying, "Not one jot, nor one tittle shall pass from the Law till all things be fulfilled"? By this He says that the Law cannot be set aside.

Why would the Word become Flesh? To say that Christ became the Word, because the Jews crucified Him, is to say that the punishment came before the crime. And it is to say that British and American law would become flesh, if Jews had crucified Him today. This is utter nonsense.

Or did the Word become Flesh because Christianity is an improvement on Judaism? This is to say also that the Civil law of the European continent is an improvement on British and American law. Few would agree with this. The world would be vastly different if the dominant religion had informed men of rule of law based on the preposition that all men are created equal. The two world wars fought to "make the world safe for democracy" might not have ever occurred if men and nations had opportunities to litigate the differences that caused them. And if there was not the tendency to dictatorship in the Continental Civil law.

Because Christians have so completely ignored Judaism, they are unaware that they believe that this Law, which rules all men and before whom all men are created equal, became a man, Jesus Christ, who rules all men, but before whom all men are not created equal. This requires that the God who created all men equal, stopped creating them equal with the birth of Christ. Since then, He created men with Original Sin who, therefore, must be baptized. Believing this, English-speaking Christians have contradicted themselves by fighting two world wars in defense of government based on the proposition that all men are created equal. By so doing, their actions say they believe that the Hebrew Law did not become Christ, that the Word did not become Flesh.

If all men are created equal before God's Law from Genesis to the present, then Christ is equal to the rest of us and He could not have worked His miracles nor risen from the dead any more than could any other man, and Christianity is not valid. If Christ was not created equal to all other men at birth, why does He indicate His equality by practicing Judaism? If at the Last Supper, when He established the New Law, He was at that moment no longer created equal, by what power did He work miracles in the previous three years? What is clear is that the Hebrew concept can't evolve into the Christian concept, and the Christian concept is a meaning forced on the Hebrew text, for the purpose of authorizing rule by an established authority: rule by Roman Canon law and eventually Civil law.

The Christian belief is that a legal system the same as American law, namely the Hebrew Law, evolved into Roman Canon law and the continental Civil law. This is to say that a legal system in which lawmaking is a function of each common citizen who votes and/or brings suit in court, evolved into a legal system in which lawmaking is the function of the sovereign and his agents. A legal system with an independent judiciary evolved into one in which the judiciary is a government agency. A legal system in which the right of trial by jury is central evolved into one in which it is almost unknown. A legal system derived from self-evident truths evolved into one derived from the dictates of one person.

3.   After Christ, these are the alternative Christian beliefs:

a) The Hebrew religion is still valid but obsolete. This is the same as saying that the British and American law is still valid, but obsolete, and that it is the Roman Canon law and Continental Civil law that are up-to-date. Few, if any, English-speaking people would accept this. And it is to say that all men are created equal, but this idea is obsolete.

Both the Hebrew and Christian concepts of the Word cannot be valid because each contradicts the other. An abstraction, such as the Word, cannot become a Person and still be an abstraction. Hebrew Law and British and American law is either what all English-speaking people know it to be, an abstraction, or it is a man who is the law. It can't be both. Therefore, if the Hebrew religion is valid today, then the Christian religion is not and never was valid, and cannot make the Hebrew concept invalid or obsolete. Until Arabic numerals were introduced to the Western world during the Crusades, this contradiction may not have been clarifiable to Christians. Rather than being obsolete, the Old Testament concept is the timeless new one—in agreement with modern law, mathematics, and science; and the New Testament concept is the old, obsolete one—from Roman numerals, science, and religion, discarded centuries ago.

b) The Hebrew religion is no longer valid. This is to say that British and American law is no longer valid, having been replaced by the person of Christ who is this law. Millions of English-speaking Christians who would instantly oppose any such man in the political sphere, attend church regularly to worship a Man who is the Law. This I suppose is because the Hebrew Law remains valid in the political sphere but is invalid in the religious sphere.

God's Law, as the Jew understands it, includes the laws of science. To say that such laws are replaced by a Man who is the Law is akin to believing that Apollo's horse-drawn chariot now moves the Sun across the sky and the Earth no longer rotates in twenty-four hours.

Let us consider what this religious difference says about who in politics should hold power and how he should use force. The nominally Christian nations of the world can be divided into two categories: those ruled by (Hebrew) law, as are the English-speaking nations, and those ruled by the Continental Civil law.

In nations ruled by the first legal system, the Jew views this law as God-given, even though its establishment has been mainly the work of non-Jews. The Christian views this law as a man-made legal system, the work of Enlightenment philosophers who based it on self-evident truths that they were able to discover. Some Christians see the contradiction between this law and Christian belief but ignore them.

In nations ruled by the Civil law in which sovereignty is centered on a dictator or on parliament, the Jew sees such rule as contradictory to the principles of Judaism. Christians see such rule as contradictory to the Enlightenment philosophy. Totalitarian regimes in such nations are seen as too harsh to be Christian. However these regimes exist, as does the Civil law, because Christians under them are impaled on the horns of a dilemma: if it is right to be ruled by a Man who is the Law in the religious sphere, then it must be right to be ruled by a man who is the law in the political sphere. If not, what is the flaw in this line of reasoning? If it is right to be ruled in the religious sphere by a Man who is his own constitution, bill of rights, judge, jury, and court of appeal, then how can this be wrong in the political sphere?

If it is right to follow Christ who set aside the Law, then it is right to follow a political leader who set aside the same law: a constitution and bill of rights. This law is only man-made, therefore, men can set it aside. But this is exactly what constitutions are instituted to prevent. It is the purpose of a constitution to be supreme and immutable, which is the meaning of "men are endowed by their Creator with certain inalienable rights." No man can set aside what the Creator has endowed, what is God-given. Unless God is invoked, a constitution is a man-made document that can be set aside by men who will be law unto thmselves as are dictators. Christians, in believing that Christ set aside the Hebrew Law, are actually believing that this Man set aside the propositions of the Constitution and Bill of Rights and installed Himself as King of Kings. But they don't realize this. He is then His own Constitution and decides which powers who will have and which rights, if any, anyone will have because He is a Man not created equal to other men.

The Christian belief, as expressed in Roman Canon law and the Continental Civil law, is that what is right or wrong originates in the decisions of those in authority. Each decides his own way, as witness the innumerable Christian denominations and the contradictions in Canon law and the Civil law in various countries. Thus rules and laws can be arbitrary, contradictory, even nonsensical and this is acceptable. Examples are the prohibition on use of alcoholic beverages and vows of celibacy required in some denominations. But since the rules are someone's invention, each man may make his own rules in imitation of Christ, and might violate the established rules as long as no one is looking. Thus corruption in government tends to exist hand in hand with belief in these irrational religious teachings.

The above is an outline of what this aspect of Christian belief says about who in politics should hold power and how he should use force. The effect of this Cristian belief is to authorize rule by a king, noble or dictator, a man who is the law, rather than rule by constitutional government. Thus constitutional government is prevented from coming into existence or if it does exist, this form of government is rendered unstable by Christian belief.

The lack of stability of constitutional governments is a most serious political problem. The March 1917 Russian Revolution established a constitutional government which lasted only until November of the same year, when it was replaced by Russian Communism. The Weimar Republic placed Germany under constitutional government only to be replaced by the dictatorship of Adolf Hitler in 1933. Constitutional government was established in Italy in 1871, and was replaced by rule of Mussolini in 1929. The recurrent instability of French constitutional government is well known. Constitutional government established in Cuba, in 1898, was replaced by Communist rule by Fidel Castro in 1959. Dictatorships alternating with constitutional rule are the familiar pattern in all of Latin America. Two world wars were fought to make the world safe for democracy, kings and nobles were deposed, only an unstable peace was achieved.

This instability is to a great extent traceable to the dilemmas listed previously, which are ultimately one dilemma. If rule of law is to be firmly established in the political sphere, it must be recognized as God-given: no man can set it aside. Which is to say that it must be firmly established in the religious sphere too. It is not sufficient to depose the kings, the King of Kings must be deposed also or rule of law established over His head.

Constitutional government in the English-speaking nations is understood also as not sufficiently stable. The violence observed through American history and on the college campus in recent years is one indication of such. A second indication is the well-known inability of the common man to discharge his duties as a juror. However, can these indications of instability be overcome through education in constitutional law without confronting these religious differences? Probably not.

Because Christians have so completely ignored Judaism, they are unaware of their predicament of having made a departure to the "improvement" on the Hebrew religion that creates these instabilities and thereby makes it impossible to attain an acceptable world peace.

Judaism provides a basis by which the common man can enter into dialogue with the heads of the many agencies that make up the modern welfare state government. Judaism requires that one's personal behavior be limited by the Law and that he be directed to the objectives and purposes inherent in this Law. This requirement has meaning not only to the individual Jew in his personal life and in his conduct as a citizen, but also to any elected official or government agency head.

The lawmaking branch of government legislates into existence government agencies for specific purposes and defines their powers. Such agencies as the military, the police force, and the highway department. Each agency should develop working policies which are statements as to how these purposes would be achieved with these powers and within legal limitation: statements as to how the administration intends to get things done. Such legislation and policies could form a basis for dialogue between each agency head and any citizen regarding any major decision to be made by the agency. This is because the policies must be based on the legislation, which, in turn, must be based on constitutional law, which, in turn, is based on self-evident truths on which all men can agree. Such dialogue does not happen because citizens are not oriented to such rule of Law by religion.

In Christianity all law is administrative law, policies—law by which the top man gets things done. There is no constitutional law based on self-evident truths to limit and separate the powers of government, no law to separate powers of legislative branch from executive branch. Therefore, there is no legislature to define powers of agencies and no separation of such legislation from working policies. All law, in being administrative law, is simply working policy, not for the most part based on self-evident truths, because, as we have seen, these self-evident truths are set aside by Christ. Thus one either accepts this man's rule or one leaves. Thus there are more denominations every year.

The above basis is an important aspect of Judaism because in modern welfare states citizens feel that they do not have enough control over their government. This is because their control is exercised primarily through the vote. They are not satisfied with feeling that they are supposed to believe in, follow, and support their man once they have voted for him, as they believe they should do with another leader. Their error is in perceiving the public official as one does the Christian authority, as without a legal basis for evaluating his conduct or entering into dialogue with him. Since Christ is seen as not subject to Law based on self-evident truths, the public officials and their constituents may see themselves as not subject either. They may feel they can set aside the law. Citizens enter into dialogue only at election time and then only with candidates, not agency heads. Because government is so vast this is deemed ineffective control.

Thus, implementation of this aspect of Judaism would require that public agencies be staffed by highly qualified people, none of whom would be permitted to hide behind some academic title or degree or other index of status, so as to avoid genuine dialogue; would require each agency head to publish its relevant enabling legislation, its policies, its major decisions and the basis for such; would urge a citizenship responsibility that would call for one to develop a high degree of knowledge about at least one public agency, so as to be able to enter into dialogue intelligently; would require much more detailed party platforms, etc. Citizens would be oriented to locating the points in the legislative process, policy-making process and agency decision-making process at which political decisions relevant to their interests are made. And citizens would be oriented to examining and criticizing the basis for such decisions. Thus Judaism would orient citizens or participation in a form of democratic government that is about as close as is practicable to direct rule by the people.

Catholicism calls for rule by the Papacy and Protestantism rule by respective Protestant authorities. Fascism, Nazism, and Communism call for rule by respective persons and their parties in imitation of Christian denominations: all not subject to rule of law. It was also thought by Christians that Judaism called for rule by Jews. And just as there is, or was, a Nazi, Fascist, and Communist conspiracy for world domination, there must be a Jewish one. This is not so, because Judaism calls for rule of Law, not rule of persons. Thus the American Constitution and Bill of Rights has never been seen for what it is, an establishment of Jewish Law, because it has never put the Jews on top. And thus the document that says, "Congress shall make no law that is an establishment of religion" has never been seen for what it is—an establishment of religion. And this establishment is what is needed to end the struggle for world domination, a religion that acknowledges the supremacy of Law, that puts law on top rather than a man, that ends this contest without rules of we versus they.

From the above, it is clear that the Christian understanding of the Jews' Bible and the accounts of Jews in the New Testament has always totally ignored the common sense understanding that the Jew placed on these texts. When we set these two contradictory understandings side by side, we can see that the Christian understanding is a meaning forced on the Hebrew texts: it is less sensible and in some ways is nonsensical compared to the Hebrew understanding. And we can also see that this forced meaning would serve the purpose of authorities in holding people down, of keeping them from using their common sense and from governing themselves under rule of law. And we can also see that there is no basis yet in our discussion for departure from the Hebrew Law and Hebrew understanding of the Bible. This is to say that there is no basis for the Canon law of the Roman Church or its offspring legal system, the Continental Civil law, as it differs from Common law.

This reason why Jews world-wide are in agreement on the

essentials of their religion is the same as our first reason. Their understanding is based on common sense in agreement with universally acceptable self-evident truths of mathematics, science, and justice.

This chapter's reason why Christians will never agree on a reasonable understanding of Christianity, is that there can be no reasonable understanding of the belief that Law becomes a Person or that a man can set aside self-evident truths of constitutional law, mathematics and science. These Christian beliefs again confirm the judgment of those who consider the religion a form of insanity, because such beliefs are unrelated to the real world. Thus the religion provides authorization for a world in which pseudo-science can be practiced, as was done by the pseudo-medical people prominent in the Nazi regime and in "medical experiments in concentration camps. If such Christian "truths" are true, then other pseudo-science could be true also, such as religious beliefs in astrology, the lost continents of Atlantis and Lemuria, etc.

Christian civilization has proceeded for centuries with the unreasonable understanding that the laws of science could be set aside. The results are that the world problems of water, air, and noise pollution have come home to roost, and there is no one who can work miracles to correct them.

This chapter is an indication of how completely Christians have found in the Bible, not the common sense that was there, but the ideas that prestigious religious authorities have said are there. These ideas provide the basis for the authority's prestige and power, their spurious right to dominate the layman and to confer status and prestige on the layman through the sacraments. One obvious cause of this religious difference is that, over the centuries, most Jews but few Christians could read and write. Therefore Christians had to be told what is in the Bible.

It is the message of this chapter that the Christian belief, "the Word was made flesh and dwelt among us," is not a mystery or a supernatural occurrence. It is simply an expression of how a Hebrew concept, the Word, became corrupted by ignorance and the lust for power that prevailed in the centuries after Christ.

Five

Abstraction: Law Becomes a Person; the Person Becomes Perfect

Still another aspect of the religious difference that follows from Law becoming a Person is that all men are equal before the Law in Judaism, in British and American law and in the law of modern mathematics and science. In Christianity this Law becomes a Person who, firstly, is not equal to all other men because He is God. Thus He is perfect. This aspect is considered in this chapter.

Secondly, before this Person all men were not created equal because those closest to Him, the celibate clergy, have, in the Medieval Church, been understood to have the right to dominate the ordinary Christian laymen. This domination was the subject of a previous chapter.

Thirdly, the Law (law) before whom all men are equal is understood to authorize rulers who have a loyal opposition. This Law becomes Christ who very clearly tolerates no opposition, because in His words, "you are either with me or against me." Those who would oppose He who is the Law are outlaws. Thus men who are equal in Judaism become unequal in Christianity because they become agents of a Man whose power is unlimited. They become members of Christ's Mystical Body. They are His arms or His legs: parts of a larger basic entity over which they have no control. This religious difference is the subject of chapter six. Those who are not members of His Mystical Body are "against" Him.

Fourthly, a Law relevant to all mankind, on which all men can unite, and before which all men are equal, is replaced by an authority whose view of the world is we versus they. *We,* in the

Medieval Church, are those who permit themselves to be dominated by the authority as parts of Christ's Mystical Body. *They* are those who historically could not be dominated: the unbaptized and such as those not "in peace and communion with the Holy See." This religious difference has been reflected in the pattern of Christian fragmentation for centuries: those not with the authority had to leave to form their own denomination. Those with the authority are morally superior to those against him. Thus each denomination also seems to have inherited the idea that it is better than any other denomination. This is also a subject of chapter six.

Fifthly, men who are equal before God's Law in Judaism are unequal in Christianity, because those who are baptized and dominated by the authority historically have occupied various moral layers approaching perfection through the imitation of Christ, with Christ Himself as perfect at the top. The celibate clergy who are closer to perfection have led the ordinary Christian layman who because of personal inadequacy is unable to embrace the celibate way of life. And he feels inferior because he is unable to do so. This aspect is considered in this chapter.

If God is a Person, then it necessarily follows that that Person is perfect. Thus, in Christianity, Christ is understood to be perfect as is His heavenly Father. Thus Christ must also be His own criterion of correctness and perfection which means He is governed by no other such criterion, such as the Hebrew Law. So Christ necessarily is the Hebrew Law, the Word made Flesh. And one approaches perfection through the imitation of Christ.

The Hebrew counterpart is that neither Christ nor any other man in Judaism is perfect, nor can anything be known about God. To be a Jew one must accept rule by the Hebrew Law. Christ in being a Jew is indicating that He does accept rule by the Law and is indicating that He is only a man equal to all the rest of us. Hence one cannot approach perfection through imitating Him.

In the common sense thought systems of Arabic numerals and the rest of modern mathematics and science, perfection is a quality only of abstract concepts, only of thoughts, not of physically existing entities. Thus from the common sense standpoint, to say that Christ is perfect is to view Him only as a thought, an ideal, an abstraction, as a figure in mythology, and never as the real living Person that He was.

Recognizing that Christianity started as a movement within Judaism, we again ask what might account for this mathematically expressible difference that is a departure from common sense. One reason why Christ became perfect is that Roman numeral mathematics expresses abstract concepts by pictures. The underlying principle is that that which is perfect, the abstract concept, can be pictured and therefore objects such as persons can be perfect. Thus the belief is the expression of the ignorance of Roman times.

A second reason why Christ becomes perfect in Christianity is that Christ personifies the perfect soldier. One cannot attain perfection as a carpenter, tent maker, tax gatherer, parent, son, or daughter because these ways of life lend themselves to too many diverse understandings. However, the perfect soldier is, in the popular understanding, he who lays down his life for his fellowman. It is he who is so charismatic that others would leave their families and follow him even unto death. It is he who is completely subject to the will of his superiors. It is he who would prove his love for his fatherland or holy mother church by enduring mutilation. It is he who sees himself in this paradisical world in which whatever he does is right as long as he is with God, because the soldier should not be concerned with the wanton evil of war. Thus the imitation of Christ and the approach to perfection is to a great extent the imitation of the virtues of a soldier. Thus to hold Christ as God is to make a god of militarism.

Thus Christ personifies the perfect soldier but only as a thought, which means that he attains perfection only after death, only in memory, only as an expendable.

A third reason why Christ becomes perfect in Christianity is that it is He who provides status and confers honors, it is He who recognizes the best people, the celibate clergy (providing authorization for similar behavior in the political sphere). His perfection is an expression of rule by the best people. The need for status and honors is keenly felt by celibates because they do not respond or give attention to the opposite sex and, therefore, they need attention as does a child from an adult. Their need is aggravated by their understanding of the Old Testament. They notice that the God of the Hebrews ignores all men except the Jews unless these non-Jews do some major violence to the Chosen. They are provoked to jealousy of the Jews and, hence, need a God up there with the God of the Hebrews who will recognize them, who will confer status on them superior to the status they perceive as Chosenness and who will keep those who provoke in their place. Thus Christ was rejected, ignored and crucified by the Jews because the celibate feels rejected, ignored, and crucified on reading the Old Testament. Central to Christianity is the idea that one is nothing without Christ, because without Christ, one is a nobody, as were the non-Jews of the Old Testament. Thus, Christ renders the Jewish Law invalid, and Christian leaders herd Jews into ghettos, if it would make the Christian feel less jealous.

Because Christians need a God up there with the God of the Hebrews, who will recognize them, an ordinary Jew is elevated to that exalted position. Thus, many Christians regard Christ as the only important Person they ever knew. He is, to them, Our Lord, as Edinburgh has its duke, Wales its prince, etc. Their first communions and confirmations, recognitions of special status before Christ, are most important events in their lives.

In the political sphere this need to be recognized by a powerful, high status person has drawn men to military service in some great general's army. The great general is a man equal to the rest of us, but his honors are coveted. His call to arms is heard. He is the perfect soldier.

In the religious sphere, to fulfill this need, an ordinary man is elevated to pope or bishop. He dispatches emissaries to even the humblest hamlets. Having created the status conferring person, the Christian develops an intolerance for anyone who speaks out against the person, especially Christ, labeling such an anti-Christ, because to speak out against the person is to speak out against the status the Christian thinks he has.

The thought pattern is that the celibate is so isolated, that he needs attention from a person. So he invents One, and invents a mythology to go with Him. The ordinary Christian has acquired something of this isolationist attitude. This need is recognized by those who design machines that accept coins at toll booths and concession stands. These flash on a lighted sign saying, "thank you" or "sorry, sold out." Who is the person who is thankful or sorry? The machine can't be thankful or sorry. There is no such person and no one seems to be aware of this, just as there is no such person as He that supposedly personifies these Hebrew concepts. But people need someone to recognize that they are doing right and they need someone to sympathize with them when they have found the machine sold out, as they need someone when they find the Old Testament "sold out" to Jews. So a Person is invented, Who is all-good and all-loving.

A fourth reason why Christ becomes perfect in Christianity is that Christ's perfection offers authorities opportunities to control people. If one denies the perfection of Christ, one denies that Christ is God, hence, one is an outcast. If one accepts the perfection of Christ, one must accept those who imitate Christ, the celibate clergy, as being perfect and as having the right to rule with Christ. And one must accept a view of humanity arranged from high status to low, to the extent such men imitate the perfection of Christ. It would follow that in the political sphere one should accept the right of the militarist to rule without criticism and to accept a view of humanity arranged in ranks from high status to low as to the extent they are perfect soldiers, expendables.

Thus criticism by the layman of the celibate clergy is dismissed as an expression of jealousy at the high status the hierarchy enjoy, especially in the eyes of women. Or as expressions of ignorance since the layman has not studied the problem for as many years. Or expressions of one "coming into court without clean hands," that is, an expression of that individual's unworthiness, lack of status, lack of perfection, lack of faith, or that that individual is not with Christ, not in the state of sanctifying grace or simply not good enough. Or expression of that individual's dissatisfaction with his own low status as a layman which is presumed to be his own fault. Those farther down have always been dissatisfied with rule by the best people, hence, force or threat of hell-fire may be needed. Hence, the Church fathers adopt a patronizing attitude to such criticism. Thus the only persons who could criticize the hierarchy would be members of the hierarchy themselves, all of whom are controlled.

Celibate rule conveys to the Christian layman that, in the ideal society, the layman never could be good enough to rule, because he is incapable of celibacy; those who are inferior can't become better.

This status view of humanity is an emotional trap, because status differences provoke jealousy. The status view requires that anyone who would want to rule, who would rise in status, must do so by imitating Christ, which in traditional Christian societies meant in effect to permit one's self to be used by the authorities: one must become a celibate with vows or a human sacrifice in the military. One must prove one is good enough to those in status by imitating He Who is all-good and by imitating those in authority. Since what is right and wrong originates in the decisions of those in authority, they set the terms by which subordinates will rise. Thus in the military all men are uniformed; the only basis for distinction are medals and ranks conferred by the authority for distinguished service. Thus a world controlled by those at the top is authorized.

The same kind of emotional trap is used in modern advertising. A single status framework, for example, that of automobile ownership, is proposed in order to provoke the customer to raise his status by buying a bigger automobile, by permitting himself to be used by the automobile retailers.

A fifth reason why Christ becomes perfect is that He together with the believer and other Gospel characters populate a mythical paradisical world in which all things are perfect or can be made so. His sins can be forgiven by confession and with the reception of the Sacrament he becomes one with Christ. Then he is right with God. It is a world needed by those who do not face reality. In this paradisical world the celibate fails to realize that his monastic cell bears great resemblance to a dungeon, that his life as a celibate is utterly empty of satisfaction, which emptiness breeds an insanely jealous mind, and that his world is corrupt with the violence of war because of his teachings. It is this world which Karl Marx called "the opium of the people." This celibate world view is opposed by a central tenet of Judaism which holds that this world is the arena for action, not for such daydreams. The subjects of these chapters: Infinity becomes limited, Law becomes a Person who then becomes a piece of bread, and so on, are suggestive of the fantasies of those under the influence of opiates.

What Christianity is, is the worship of an idealization of one's self as perfect by those who do not accept their real selves, the celibate clergy, and those who imitate them. They do not accept their real selves because no one of the opposite sex accepts them. This pattern was inherited from mythological worship. Pagan houses of worship such as the Pantheon in Rome were converted into Christian Churches and thus the old behavior pattern continued. Christ took on the image of what is ideal to the worshipper: his own self and his own people, which is why Christ is sexless. Each sees Him as himself or herself. The image of the respective worshipper can be seen in countless statuary over the world: there is a Black madonna and Child, a Korean one, a Chinese, Malaysian, and Nordic one, because Christ is the idealization of the worshipper. There is every race represented except that which Mary and Jesus were: Semitic Jews, dark skinned and dark haired, because Jews don't worship Christ. All such mythology and self-worship are forbidden in Judaism by the Graven Image Commandment.

The celibate has withdrawn into this mythical paradisical world, in which he approaches perfection, as a jealous reaction. The mythology of the New Testament is created because the Jews in this world have the mythological status the celibate wants. He takes vows of celibacy, because the girls have what he wants. He takes vows of poverty, because the marketplace sells what he wants. And he takes vows of obedience, because the ordinary man has the freedom he wants. And he creates a belief world, because he wants the knowledge the intellectual has. He creates a hierarchy, because he wants the status others have. Because he wants the sexual opportunities of the younger men, he demands vows of celibacy and sets out severe restrictions on sexual expression even in marriage. Because he wants the clothing and homes of other men, a barrackslike monastic existence is ideal. By all this he proves that he doesn't want what he wants. His world is one corrupted by jealousy brought on by the celibate state.

Let us again consider the Christian beliefs below in light of this clarification of the religious difference.

1. Before Christ, these are the alternative Christian beliefs:

a) The Hebrew religion was valid.

This means that neither Christ nor any other man in Judaism was perfect nor could anything be known about God. The Hebrew Law was the final criterion of correctness.

b) The Hebrew religion was valid but the Christian belief was valid also.

This belief ignores the parallels of the old pagan worship to Christian worship, and that the Old Testament is an account of how Judaism is differentiated from this pagan worship. This belief means that no one could be perfect, but Christ and His blessed Mother could be perfect, if they had been born. This is an obviously impossible position, maintained by confronting reality to a limited extent and entertaining mythology in the same instant. The belief means also that nothing could be known about God but it could be known that God, who should be imitated, has the personality of a soldier—an expendable.

2. At some time during Christ's life the Christian religion became valid and is valid today. At that time Christ became perfect.

This raises first the question as to when Christ became perfect. The Gospel account that Christ informed His apostles of His divinity only at the Last Supper, indicates that He was perceived by all those around Him at least until that time as another human being, that is, as no more perfect than anyone else. He is perceived as only human by the Roman soldiers who crucified Him the following day. He dies because He is only human, not perfect. Christ remains human. He never does become perfect in the thought system of Judaism, modern mathematics and science. Thus He becomes perfect only in the minds of those influenced by Roman numeral mathematics and mythology, those to whom Christ serves a psychological need. If Christ's actual teachings were that He is divine and, therefore, perfect, why does He contradict Himself by practicing the Hebrew Law and dying on the cross which necessarily indicate that He is not perfect?

The second question, related to the first, is, when did the militaristic themes that we have found incorporated into Christian belief become valid? What happened is that the story of Christ's life embraced militaristic themes in a less harsh sense than the previous pagan mythologies, so that the religion centered on Christ replaced these harsher mythologies, and the old habits of self-worship and "we versus they" attitude continued. No attention ever was given to the invalidity of these themes in Judaism.

3. After Christ, these are the alternative Christian beliefs:

a) The Hebrew religion is still valid but obsolete.

The Hebrew understanding of the lack of perfection of persons is the common sense one in agreement with modern mathematics. If it is obsolete, then common sense and modern mathematics are obsolete too, as is the idea of rule by the common people. Since common sense and modern mathematics are still valid, Christ is not perfect except in an imaginary, "make it up as you go along," sense. The New Testament concept of perfection of real objects is the old obsolete one, discarded along with the rest of Roman numerals about eight hundred years ago.

b) The Hebrew religion is no longer valid.

This is to say that the principle that only abstract concepts can be perfect holds true in all spheres of knowledge except the religious sphere, in which it once was true but is no longer. In that sphere, men are urged "be ye perfect as your heavenly Father is perfect." Again Christians are in the predicament of having made a departure from a common sense understanding of the Jews' Bible to a position that is nonsensical and indefensible, because they have so completely ignored Judaism.

Let us consider what follows in the political sphere from this religious difference. The self-worship aspects of Christianity provide authorization for the nationalism that is familiar to all students of the history of Christian civilization. The worship of He who is perfect holds it ideal to see one's self as perfect, it is to be unwilling to admit any imperfection in one's self. In such a we-versus-they world, differences between nations can thus be settled only by war because the only difference that is to be settled is whether they submit to our perfection, to the rightness of our cause.

Rule by Christ who has no loyal opposition provides authorization for similar dictatorial rule in the political sphere. Thus Christians in such nations are impaled on the horns of the dilemma.

Rule by He who personifies the perfect soldier provides authorization for similar rule in the political sphere, without loyal opposition, in a hierarchy descending from such a person, each man superior to subordinates in military qualities. In such a society the top man or his agents confer titles or medals on subordinates. In sum, a militaristic society is authorized.

The celibate's world corrupted by jealousy provides authorization for a society in which men are uniformed and regimented as in a monastery or army so that individual differences which could provoke jealousy do not show. And as ideal an economy in which the means of production of wealth and all employment are controlled by the state. And in which knowledge of the party philosophy and membership in the party are more important than knowledge based on common sense. Such a society is one in which authorities should control people to keep people from doing what would make other people jealous.

People cannot unite against the authority in such a society because then they would lose the status conferred on them by the authority. Of this status they are very jealous. A second reason they cannot unite is that they are isolated from one another and lack insight into one another's personalities and motives, as are the celibate clergy. Therefore, a blood, racial mystical relationship is invoked. In the religious sphere this relationship is the Mystical Body of Christ. In the political sphere master race and nationalistic concepts are invoked. It is a world in which people are of different levels of status, in which the lower levels are understood to be not worthy, are not good enough. This is a well-known Christian theme and is very prominent in Hitler's *Mein Kampf* and his reputed last words.

Individual citizens in totalitarian nations accept certain policies of their governments because these policies are expressions of the jealousies and daydreams of individuals. The murder of the upper classes in Russia and the institution of an ideal society called a "workers' paradise" subsequent to 1917 has its parallel in Hitler's murder of intellectuals and Jews (since all Jews are rich) and his promise of *Lebensraum*. Thus individual jealousy gives rise to jealousy expressed as an internal government policy and also as an international policy, as members of the Mystical Body, and the body politic. Thus before World War I, France and England had colonies, Germany was jealous and wanted them.

One detects in Nazism, Fascism, and Communism the fantasies needed by those who were or are jealous of the high standard of living enjoyed in Western Europe and North America. The fantasies also authorize a state of mind conducive to the individual's exploitation as a worker and soldier. Thus the educated and leisure classes and the Jews under such regimes must be exterminated or else have their privileges curtailed. We must sacrifice to prove that we don't want the material goods readily available to others. We must therefore lead a Spartan existence. Our reward will come in the Workers Paradise or Lebensraum promised us, as Christianity promises Heaven. Hence ideas of a Master Race and decadent Wall Street imperialism have great appeal. Hence there shall be a lack of communication with those of whom one is jealous, as there has been a lack of communication between Jews and Christians. Therefore an Iron Curtain is rightfully erected. And hence in the works of Lenin there is much patent nonsense which serves the purpose of glorifying the working man. Hence Russian propaganda claims so many Western inventions were made by Russians. Hence these movements are intolerant of those who would speak out against the nation's leaders. Hence also Cuba, the foreign nation most often visited by Americans in search of a good time, is the first in the Western Hemisphere to go Communist. One root of the problem is the authorization in Christianity to create a fantasy when one is jealous rather than accept one's real self.

Christ as the perfect soldier, authorizes an orientation to militarism on the part of those who would imitate him. He also authorizes a political leadership that imitates Him in such as the ways below. These political leaders were able to do such because Christians in those nations were impaled on the horns of the dilemma: that what is right in the religious sphere must be right in the political sphere. Thus the ideal leader has contempt for law and due process as Christ had contempt for the Hebrew Law —as, for example, Stalin's contempt for a treaty as a "scrap of paper," Hitler's contempt for the Soviet-German Pact of 1939 by his invasion of Russia in 1941, and his contempt for parliamentary rule. The ideal leader, as did Christ, heaps scorn on Jews. He is anti-Semitic. The ideal leader, in imitation of Christ, is held up for imitation and for flattery, since imitation is the sincerest form of flattery.

Six

Abstraction: Law Becomes a Person; the Individual Becomes One with That Person in the Mystical Body

In Christianity the God of the Hebrews becomes the First Person of the Trinity and the Law or Word of God becomes the Person of Christ. The relevant purpose of this Law before which all men are created equal, is to limit the power of religious and political authorities, and to prevent the centralization of such authority. And so Judaism remains a family-type religion without a central authority. The rabbi remains a lawyer equal to all other men but possessing special knowledge of the Law. To say that this Law can become a Man, or can be set aside by a Man, before Whom all men are no longer equal, is to defeat this purpose of limiting power.

In British and American law, this purpose has been achieved in a constitution to limit and separate the powers of government, and a bill of rights to protect the people from misrule. In Britain the powers of the Crown are separated into those held by the prime minister, parliament, and the king's courts. The prime minister and parliament are each a check on the other's power and the people are a check on the power of both. In the courts, the function of the jury is to prevent interference or control of the decision by political leaders. In the United States the three branches are called the executive, legislative and judicial. The prime minister or executive, as the government, requests legislation and the parliament, congress or legislature, representing the people, consents or does not consent. Men are free to form political parties with others of the same political persuasion. They may join the one in power or one out of power but loyal to the law: the loyal opposition. Such is the nature of government by consent of the governed. It begins with law above the king or authority limiting and separating his powers.

The laws of mathematics and science also limit the powers of authorities religious and political. These laws inform people that no one can work miracles, no one can claim powers by working miracles and that all men are equal before these laws. In Christianity, these laws are set aside by Christ and by the priest who works the miracle of turning bread and wine into the body and blood of Christ.

Christ the King as the Law, or in setting aside the Law, is very clearly authorizing political and religious rule that is without limitation except by He Himself. He authorizes kings and popes who rule by divine right, as He rules. He does not authorize government by consent of the governed because He leaves no law over His head in Christianity authorizing such consent or separation of His powers into branches that consent or do not consent or that authorize a bill of rights to protect His followers from misrule. The Law that limits and then separates the powers of any king becomes Christ the King in Christianity.

He is His own final authority as to how His powers will be separated or limited, if at all, because He has all the power (which He demonstrates by working miracles).

Thus men who are free under Judaism can be reduced in Christianity to being Christ's agents or His arms, twenty-four hours a day, because there is no law over His head to limit His powers.

Thus, Law, in Judaism, that makes men free becomes, in Christianity, law which can be used by the top man to control people—law by which He gets things done: administrative or disciplinary law. This leaves no law to which to appeal against misrule by Christ the King. He is His own final authority as to whether or not He misrules. Because Christ is God he is perfect, therefore He never misrules. Christians in totalitarian nations are impaled on the horns of this dilemma: if it is right to be so ruled without appeal law in the religious sphere, then it must be right to be so ruled in the political sphere. If not, what is the flaw in this line of reasoning?

The above legal effects were historically institutionalized in the Mystical Body of Christ and the sacrament of the Holy Eucharist. In this body a celibate clergy are the head and the laymen the body. In this body the Christian does not relate to the weak, he becomes one body and one blood with Christ, who is all-powerful. He becomes His agent or arm. He becomes subject to control by the head, subject to administrative or disciplinary law. Being one with Christ a celibate clergy is referred to as being the "bride of Christ." The Church as a body is also the bride of Christ. This Mystical Body is the New Covenant in which men share in the blood Christ shed for the remission of sins. As in His words, "Unless you eat my body and drink my blood, you shall not enter the kingdom of heaven," and, "unless a man be born of water and blood, you shall not enter . . ." indicate that men should see themselves as part of Christ's body, as children of God being born. These teachings are expressions that one is nothing without Christ and the sacraments—nothing except what a big man makes one—as the soldier is nothing without his general and his army.

This embodiment of abstraction is alien to Judaism. The Israelites are never conceived as forming one body whether in Moses, Solomon, or the God of the Hebrews. Nor are Israelites the bride of Moses or anyone else. Moses had his own bride, which was then a matter of some controversy. Nor has Judaism ever had any authority—as the pope—who is the Jewish community or who is Judaism, or who is the temple or synagogue. Judaism remains an idea, an abstraction that has no visible expression to Jews. It is only in Christianity that Judaism is equated with Jews. Thus Christians say that Jews do not accept the divinity of Christ, and ignore whether or not Judaism could be reconciled with the divinity of Christ. And thus there is the Christian belief that Judaism was rendered invalid by the Jews crucifying Christ. And thus there is this Christian idea in Nazism: there will be no Judaism if there are no Jews.

In no sense are Jews all of one ancestor, one blood. Some

Jews are descended from their biblical ancestors, others are Russians converted about eight hundred years ago and still others, such as the black Jews of Ethiopia, are of origin unknown.

To believe that God has a body to which men are joined is a violation of the Graven Image Commandment. Each Jew is joined to his God in a Covenant, the terms of which require him to keep God's Laws guaranteeing freedom and liberty, and which limit his behavior to that which is self-evidently right or wrong (to an informed common sense understanding of what is right or wrong). The Covenant has no visible expression. It is an idea. It was not even written down until twenty-six hundred years ago. No organization other than the family can arise out of it. Thus, the Jew is an independent citizen. (However Jews are urged to associate with a temple or synagogue.) This Covenant becomes the Mystical Body, the New Covenant, meaning that the terms of the Old Covenant became a relationship between a god-man and Christians that is without terms other than those set by the Christian authority.

Men under the Old Covenant are ruled by laws guaranteeing the liberty of the individual. Under the New Covenant, men do not have individual liberty: they are born into a part of a larger organism, which already had a head, as they are born from a larger organism into a family that already has a head.

Recognizing that the Hebrew concept of Law and the Covenant is the original one, we ask why Christians personify its counterpart and the body of Christians by the Mystical Body. In addition to the Roman numeral basis for this kind of thinking, Athens was personified by Athena, Britain by Britannia, and in modern times the United States by Uncle Sam and Britain by John Bull. General DeGaulle personified France in his statement, "I am France." Hitler personified his armies in the statement, "Hitler invaded Russia in 1941." All these are groups of people, bodies politic personified by one. Centuries ago, France, Spain, and England referred to these nations' monarchies and today Uncle Sam also refers to the federal government. The government and its people are one body. In accord with this pattern of thinking, a celibate clergy personify Law and the Covenant by a blood relationship because this is their expression of their relationship to others: they see all others in their church as blood relations. All women are seen as sisters: that is, not as sex objects. Hence, also, in the religious life there are the titles of father, mother, brother, and sister. But this expression   of a relationship is an expression of a lack of a genuine relationship. It is an expression of isolation. He who has a father or brother, or friend in as many places as there are such religious has never known what it is to have a father, brother, or friend.

Having defined this religious difference that has a mathematical expression let us consider what differences follow in the religious sphere.

The Mystical Body is a conception of an organization in which Christians are one with Christ. Christ is the head and followers are the body: parts of a larger basic entity that has a previously defined purpose: to serve the head and to be controlled by it. Each part has its right place and should, of course, stay in it. It is Christ's body: it belongs to Him, just as it is Christ's Church. The followers do not own it or control it because they do not control him. The best people—the celibate clergy— the hierarchy form the head and the ordinary Christian is an arm of this body controlled by the head. When one is in the state of grace and has received the Holy Eucharist, one is one body and blood with Christ and one is right with God. In effect, in the Mystical Body an individual is one with Christ in a military, economic, political, communal, and emotional sense.

These aspects are taken up in some detail in the following pages. As one reads these aspects it will become increasingly difficult to remember that the Mystical Body is believed to be the New Covenant, to have evolved out of the Old Covenant. It will be seen that the Mystical Body and the Holy Eucharist are institutionalizations encrusted with age of the corruptions of absolute power. The absolute power that comes from setting aside the Law that limits the powers of the King.

The Mystical Body is central to Protestant-Catholic differences. In Catholicism, one's approach to God is always through the Church. One is a part; one cannot stand before God alone separate from the Mystical Body as is the Protestant claim. Paralleling this difference are the attitudes toward the headship of the Papacy.

Thus a legal relationship between God and man that requires one to rationally understand God's Law is believed to evolve into what is in effect a military relationship. In the Mystical Body, Christians march as soldiers in one body as if they are part of Christ's army. This militaristic aspect is expressed in many hymns such as *"Onward Christian Soldiers"* and in Confiirmation which makes one a soldier of Christ. They march to attain glory as Christ attained such through His passion, death, and resurrection. Thus, in the Gospel account, Jews working in the marketplace are called to be members of Christ's band, to follow him to the ends of the earth, not for money but for distinctions He may confer on them. Thus in the religious life, one leads a barrackslike existence in return for great but unseen spiritual rewards or perhaps distinction as a monsignor or bishop—as the militarists offer glory, medals for valor, or commission as a sergeant or captain. Thus, the Medieval Papacy appointed bishops, priests, and so forth, much as a military leader would appoint colonels, captains and lieutenants. The Papal powers are separated into religious orders as the militarist's were separated into cavalry, foot soldiers, lancers, and bowmen. Thus the Jesuits are referred to as the pope's shock troops. The Papacy's opposition is excommunicated or herded into ghettos as have been the Jews.

The Mystical Body and the Holy Eucharist are institutionalizations of the idea that one is nothing without Christ—that if one separates one's self from the sacraments, one has lost everything, by which is meant eternal life, glory in heaven. The aspect is militaristic. One cannot attain glory as a soldier outside the general's army. Regarding the development of one's own talents and abilities: this concept provides authorization for the attitude that one need not make anything of himself in any way unrelated to Christ. Thus one need only develop his talents as, for example, a bowman or cavalryman: those talents that make one into a means to a goal defined by the leader, and not those talents that would make one an independent citizen. Thus personal identity is not to be achieved through self-development or by the quality of one's personal life. It is achieved by being part of a group, by being a Jesuit, a Franciscan, as other men are Marines and Commandos. This aspect is still prominent in the Roman and Greek Orthdox Churches but is greatly diluted elsewhere. It has its obvious authorization in the Gospels in which the apostles and disciples are nothing without Christ and are urged to ignore their personal preferences in a wife, family, and home to follow Him. Christ, who as God is perfect, is not seen as having developed his personal tastes and preferences, so why should those who profess to imitate Him? Those He chose as followers were simple and unlettered. Also, inherent in the idea that God became Man in the Person of Christ, whom all should love, is to require that people not express their personal preferences in their choice of a leader. If people did express themselves, Christ's popularity could be expected to rise and fall as does that of any celebrity of the day.

Education in such a society tends to be indoctrination, because one is simply to be trained to be an agent, an arm of the Mystical Body.

This legal relationship in Judaism is also believed to become an emotional relationship with Christ and His Mystical Body, which is a meaning of "the Church is the bride of Christ." Thus the stations of the cross ask us to share with Christ the torment of His crucifixion and death, and as the Easter season approaches, anti-Semitism rises also. This emotional relationship is a theme of many Christian hymns and provides authorization in the political sphere for military spirit and traditions. The new recruit, as the newly confirmed, should inherit the spirit of his regiment which carried it to victory in the last engagement and which calls for seeking revenge for defeats inflicted generations or centuries ago on the body politic, the fatherland, as the Jews could never be forgiven for what they did to Christ.

More specifically, the Christian theme is an expression of the common man's emotional involvement with military leaders that is very prominent in European history. One should follow Christ as soldiers followed such leaders. The involvement has its obvious moral authorization in the Gospels. The apostles and disciples have such a strong emotional charismatic attachment to Christ, that they would leave their families to win souls for Christ. This emotional attachment is complemented by a deprecation of the emotional ties that bind fathers and husbands to children and wives. For example, the holy family is centered not on the husband-wife relationship, because that, according to belief, was celibate, but on the mother-child relationship of Jesus and Mary. Madonna and Child are emphasized in countless statuary, holy days and church names. The husband and wife relationship of Joseph and Mary is eclipsed. Fatherhood and husbandhood are deprecated by making Joseph, who according to belief was neither a real father or a real husband, the ideal father and husband. And in the parable of the wedding feast, he who said, "I have married a wife, pray hold me excused," is deprecated. The lesson is clear: one's first love and loyalty should be to the leader of the band of Christ; one should be ready to leave home at all times to follow Him.

Thus the Mystical Body is the expression of a blood Covenant, a blood brotherhood, that could be expected from a celibate clergy. To hold celibacy as an ideal is to hold the dreams and aspirations that are naturally a part of love and affection between the sexes as having their ideal expression not in courtship and marriage, but in religious and political organizations and activity. The latter expressions are called religious and political romanticism. Christ's words prohibiting thoughts of lust, in effect, hold it ideal for the young man to dream of conquest, glory, surrender, and impregnating the impregnable on the battlefield rather than on the marital bed. And to dream of holding a person down as a member of Christ's band of preachers rather than in bed. And to become emotionallly involved with a great military leader rather than with a member of the opposite sex. In sum, to desire power or be an instrument of somone's lust for power rather than to desire the opposite sex.

Christ's prohibitions are understood to authorize a celibate clergy: individuals who establish no emotional ties to anyone of the opposite sex and who also abandon their attachment to their families. Such emotional ties should be directed only to Christ. And it authorizes a Christian home, like those of the apostles: centered on a god-man outside the home. The function of the home is to provide men for the band of followers of Christ. This is a vast departure from Judaism which is centered on the home that does not have the function of providing members for any band.

In Judaism there is no leader with whom Jews are or were emotionally involved, because the prohibition against lustful thoughts, so prominent in Christianity, is hardly emphasized in Judaism. And because emotional involvement with the leader or the body politic tends to obscure awareness by followers that their rights are being trampled upon.

A legal relationship in Judaism, the Covenant, is also believed to become a moral relationship with Christ and the Mystical Body: men are right or wrong to the extent they are with Christ, to the extent they receive the sacraments and are in sanctifying grace. In the Mystical Body, Christians share collectively in guilt and in graces earned by the saints (the communion of saints), in some mystical sense. That the Church forms one conscience is the concept underlying the sacrament of Confession: the body must purify its parts by absolution and reception of the Eucharist. Men are guilty in a body as the whole human race is guilty of Original Sin, without ever having been tried or convicted. All Jews are guilty for crucifying Christ. The whole world is guilty before Christ is a message of Christian preachers. Thus men should feel guilty (morally inadequate) until proved innocent or made innocent through Baptism or other sacraments. (This authorizes the guilty until proved innocent principle of Roman Canon law and the Continental Civil law. It holds people down by making them feel guilty if they oppose the authorities.) Christ's graces, earned through His passion and death, redeem all men and reopen the gates of heaven. The sacrifices and prayers of the saints provide graces by which all Christians can resist temptation to sin.

The Mystical Body conception provides authorization in the political sphere for the familiar views that men are guilty in bodies politic as, for example, the "German soldier" is guilty for having invaded France and Russia. In war it is not important to punish the specific enemy soldiers who committed the last atrocity. One should attempt to kill the next enemy one sees. If the enemy appears, one does not recognize his right of trial by jury, one shoots him on sight. He is guilty without a trial. Therefore, once the Jews had been defined as enemies of the state by the Hitler regime, it was justifiable to murder them without a trial. All were rightly retaliated against, even children. It is a world in which, because everyone is guilty collectively, no one is guilty and, therefore, blame for any wrongdoing can be passed upwards, downwards, sideways, front or back to other members in the ranks of Christ's band.

The Mystical Body provides authorization for the view that one race is morally superior to another if a few of its members have contributed more to civilization, produced more Nobel Laureates, etc. And for the view that one is better because he is a blood relative of one who is wealthier, better educated, of higher birth, etc. Basic to such a view is the idea that all members of one blood share in these achievements in some mystical sense, as all Jews share in guilt. Thus the Mystical Body provides authorization for the worst expressions of bigotry. Thus those who are inferior can't become better. As those who had a Jewish ancestor back to the fourth generation could not be admitted into the Jesuit order. As even if Jews became Christians they remained morally inferior and were eradicated by Hitler.

The Hebrew Law is a statement of truths with a message relevant to all mankind, such as "all men are created equal." As this Law becomes a Person, these truths are seen as becoming limited in application to one's fellow members of the Mystical Body rather than to all mankind. This is because these statements of truth are replaced by statements based on the authority's view of the world in a we-versus-they framework. And secondly, these truths were replaced historically by ideas developed from the ordinary Christian's view of himself as a part. That is, the tendency in Christianity is to make virtues such as loyalty, courage, honesty, gallantry, humility, and helpfulness of value only as they relate to Christ and His band of followers: only as they relate to the purposes of an organization as defined by the leaders, only as they relate to one's own people. Thus Negroes were not admitted into white people's churches. Thus the Jesuit professed take an oath of personal obedience to the Pontiff and the vows of religious are related to organizational purposes. Therefore, the oath of obedience Hitler required of his followers compelled them to commit the most heinous crimes against non-Germans, because it could not be violated. Thus through history, Christian charity was not owed to Jews and heathens, or even to other Christian denominations, because they are not "our people." Therefore the Jews must take shelter in Israel because they are not safe in Christian Europe. And "Christian" treatment of the heathen and so-called inferior races has been notoriously inhumane for centuries.

1.   Before Christ, these are the alternative Christian beliefs:

a) The Hebrew religion was valid. Then as today Jews were joined in a Covenant with their God, which required that they keep His Laws and in return He would reward them by making them a great nation. The nation clearly would be ruled by law as are the English-speaking peoples and modern Israel: law limiting the power of religious and political authorities. Also, He would confound the Jews' enemies. He would send a Messiah. He would make the Jews' enemies their footstool.

b) The Hebrew religion was valid but the Law and the Covenant were actually the Mystical Body of Christ. However, this had not yet been revealed. If so, it is impossible to understand how the Jews developed their ideas, expressed in the Bible about the Covenant and God's promise, which do not at all resemble a body.

2.   At the Last Supper, Christ instituted the New Covenant which is valid today.

The Hebrew Law and Covenant became the Mystical Body. It is difficult to understand how a contractual obligation between God and man, like thousands of other contracts made through history, could evolve into such a thing, least of all when Christ still inhabited His own body. Also, Christ's body never is available to become this Mystical Body. On resurrection day it is missing from the tomb and is replaced by the Risen Christ, which is not His body, because it appears and disappears. This Christian belief confirms the judgment of some people that the religion is a form of insanity. Secondly, the belief says that a contract with terms and conditions stated in the Bible evolves into a noncontractual relationship without terms and conditions. Thirdly, the promise of a great nation ruled by the Hebrew Law is actually a promise to make the entire world free, as freedom is understood in the English-speaking nations. The Christian belief is that this promise has evolved into political and religious bureaucracies that effectively hold people down.

In Judaism the adherent enters into dialogue with God based on the principles of God's Law. The Christian belief is that this situation evolved into one in which one's approach to God is only through the Church. Emotional involvement with the opposite sex is replaced by emotional involvement ideally with great religious and political leaders of the same sex. A religion in which there is great emphasis on rights and liberties evolves into one in which emotional involvement obstructs awareness of one's rights and liberties.

3. After Christ, these are the alternative Christian beliefs:

a) The Hebrew religion is still valid but obsolete. If still valid, then the Covenant still holds. It has not evolved into a Mystical Body any more than has any other contract. And the Christian religion is not valid. Therefore it cannot make the Hebrew religion invalid or obsolete. (Both religious concepts cannot be valid because each contradicts the other.) Also the entire Christian world should now be ruled by law in the British and American tradition, and ruled by the Hebrew Law in the religious sphere. All with a level of political stability perhaps approximating that of the modern democracies, if the Hebrew religion is valid. But this idea should be considered obsolete.

In the political sphere this idea is anything but invalid or obsolete. It is a goal toward which many people have worked, starting before the establishment of the old League of Nations and continuing with the United Nations. Again this Old Testament concept of what Judaism offers is the new modern one and the New Testament concept is another old obsolete one from Roman mythology and militarism.

b) The Hebrew religion is no longer valid. This holds that the great nation ruled by law in the British and American tradition that has been promised the Jews never will exist, because people are Christians; because it has evolved into rule by a Man who is the Law and whose headship is as the head is to the body. Citizens are simply parts of His nation as His arm is part of His body. And this holds that there is no solution in law to world political problems except nuclear war, which is not a solution either.

The above indicates that when we place the Hebrew concept beside the Christian concept, we can see that the latter does not evolve out of the former and that the Christian concept is an unrelated meaning forced on the Hebrew concept for the purpose of controlling people. It is perhaps a meaning that evolves out of a state of mind characteristic of the ancient Roman or Medieval Church. The Hebrew meaning has been corrupted by the ignorance and lust for power of Roman times.

Thus another reason why Christians will never agree on a reasonable understanding of the religion is again because there is none. A contract can't become a mystical body and again the judgment of those who say the Christian religion is a form of insanity would appear to be confirmed. A family-type religion, which Judaism is, can't evolve into one that authorizes religious and political romanticism, except in celibate mentalities. The extent to which Christians are informed by this kind of thinking is the extent they can be relieved of their rights and be persuaded to follow a military adventurer. And this has been particularly characteristic of Germans, Frenchmen and Spaniards.

Again, if it is right to view one's self as do Christians in the religious sphere, people through history have concluded that it must be right to view one's self as the same in the political sphere. And so the religion has existed for centuries with a body politic whose members were part of a military machine. As Christ personifies the Church and should be imitated, so the head of state personifies the nation and should be imitated. But the head of state has the power to use force, because that is the function of government. Therefore, since everyone should imitate he who has the power to use force, it is right for everyone to belong to the military or police arm of the government, to belong to someone's war machine. Hence, Christ personifies the soldier, the expendable. We have again stated the dilemma of Christians in totalitarian nations. In the Third Reich, the Mystical Body was expressed in the sentence, "Hitler is Germany—Germany is Hitler."

Because the citizen viewed himself as a part, rulers could make the secret treaties that are widely regarded as a major cause of World War I. And at the peace tables of two world wars demands such as these were in order: Russia wants all of Poland east of the Curzon Line; Poland wants Bukovina; France wants Alsace-Lorraine and so on. In each case, the nation conceives itself as one body with a policy of self-aggrandizement and a policy of bullying other nations, because international law is nonexistent. Men must see themselves as parts of such bullies and those men who do not fit in, such as the Jews, are chased from one nation to another. And this has been history. In this world, men could be free and independent only in insular nations such as England, Ireland, Norway, Sweden, Switzerland, United States, Canada, Australia, New Zealand. For the citizens of other nations to be free and independent, all nations must move to rule of law. And this is the predicament of modern Israel. The Jews of Israel accept rule of law internally but could not act internationally as if rule of law existed, because it does not. Thus, these nations require military service, recognizing that it is a violation of constitutional rights.

This concept of a mystical body politic obstructs recognition that a free society does not have collective national goals toward which men should march in one body, other than goals that would assure freedom for all, such as universal free education. Freedom in a free society is freedom not to be an arm of government, such as a member of the armed forces. Recognizing this, the English-speaking nations cannot be truly free societies until world rule of law establishes world peace.

The right of trial by jury is an expression of the liberty of the individual in the Hebrew, British and American law. Basic to such right, which is not recognized under the Canon law of the Roman Church and the Continental Civil law, is the understanding that men are not parts of a larger basic entity. In the Mystical Body, the court, as are all men, is an agent of the sovereign, be he pope, king, or a parliament. Trial by jury is, therefore, simply packing the court with more agents of the sovereign, where one, the judge, will do.

The idea that all men should be one blood with Christ provides authorization for the same conception of the state: that citizens should be one blood with their rulers (of the same racial, ethnic or national background. This is an understanding of the nature of blood before the advent of modern science and blood transfusion). Those who are one blood with the ruler are better than those who are not, as those who receive Christ are better than those who do not. Again one can see clearly that the Hebrew concept was corrupted by this scientific ignorance in Roman times. This Christian concept authorizes a division of men into categories along presumed blood lines: as Ephesians, Hebrews, Galatians, Thessalonians, Romans and so on. In America this kind of thinking has almost disappeared except for laws against intermarriage between Whites and Negroes in our Southern states, but it has great prominence in Hitler's writings. Everywhere he sees blood. And he sees that this authorizes preservation of the species as a purpose of the state which in turn presupposes a spirit of sacrifice in the individual for this purpose (in imitation of Christ). Therefore it is right for such a state to fight for living space, at the expense of other races. Hitler's purge of Germany along "blood" lines is well known as is his achievement of Anschluss: the union of all Germans in one body politic, and his regard for the American states as having been bastardized and, therefore, weakened by intermarriage, none of which conceptions, including the Mystical Body, have a scientific basis.

In Nazi Germany, Aryans were seen as of one blood, one race, and Jews as of another. "Aryan" can be recognized as a secularization of "Christian." Jews were exterminated as a race based solely on religion, not a blood type, curvature of nose, or other physical characteristic.

This same idea, because it required proportional representation in legislative bodies, must take a large share for having made representative government unworkable on the Continent. In national congresses each ethnic group was given seats in proportion to its population, because people viewed themselves as inherently different along these presumed blood lines. Voting of each ethnic group as a body occurred. This meant that one party or coalition nearly always won and the others nearly always lost. This reduced the losers to second-class citizenship. To make the legislative process work men must see themselves in a different context: each man as a free independent citizen; all men as created equal. Hitler writes of this situation in Austria before World War I with great contempt: Jews, Czechs, Slovaks, and Hungarians were foreign bodies in the body politic, because it was a German nation with a German king.

Again, because Christians have so completely ignored Judaism, they are unaware of their predicament of having made a departure from a common sense understanding of the Bible to an "improvement on Judaism" that is highly disruptive of parliaments as well as world peace.

A law set up to make men free, evolving into a bureaucracy that holds people down, is the way some see many features of the modern welfare state, not only in the free world but under Communism. This is because the Christian religion authorizes rule by a bureaucracy where rule of law is sufficient and, thus, obstructs awareness that government bureaucracy is a necessary evil. Public education has as its purpose education for citizenship in a free society, but some feel that the highly intelligent, the Negro, the Puerto Rican, and other minorities are suppressed by the bureaucracy. Laws set up to provide public housing are seen as authorizing an authority that constructs and maintains barracks-type housing, thus telling people how to live. Some welfare programs are seen as permitting bureaucrats to regulate the sex lives of recipients, as the bureaucracies of some churches have regulated the sex lives of the laymen.

In the political sphere Christian themes provide authorization for a militaristic society. The most important function of the home is to provide members of the military. This function does not disrupt home life, because home should be centered on the mother-child relationship as it was in the holy family. When duty calls, one should never let one's home life interfere. Those who followed Napoleon and other adventurers did because it was their understanding of Christianity that it is right to do so, that he who would remain at home with his wife and family should be deprecated.

Whatever the nature of the Apostles' emotional tie to Christ, whether it be like that between father and son, or if it be like that emotional tie that teenagers often have on an older member of the same sex, or whether it be like that of a wife who must follow her husband wherever he goes, without question (the Church is the bride of Christ), it is very clear that this tie is not that of consent to be governed of people who are conscious of the right to govern themselves. It is a relationship without terms. A vastly different relationship to one's leaders is characteristic of citizens in a free society, which the Mystical Body is not and cannot be. If I say, "I think Jesus Christ was a liar," millions of English-speaking Christians would take personal offense. The same remark made about Winston Churchill,

President Roosevelt or President Eisenhower would bring no such reaction, because the Christian is emotionally involved only with Christ.

This aspect authorizes emotional involvement with the body politic: a chauvinistic nationalism, very familiar to any student of European history. Such involvement is extremely intense in Hitler's *Mein Kampf*. He is a part of the Fatherland and is emotionally involved in it as a soldier in World War I, in the national dream of achieving the Anschluss: the union with Austria of all Germans in a single body politic, and in the stab-in-the-back legend accounting for defeat in that war: the nation had one back to be stabbed. He expresses this emotional involvement in the following:

> "But finally I wanted to enjoy the happiness of living and working in the place which some day would inevitably bring about the fulfillment of my most ardent and heartfelt wish: the union of my beloved homeland with the common fatherland, the German Reich.
>
> "Even today many would be unable to comprehend the greatness of such a longing, but I address myself to those to what Fate has either hitherto denied this, or from whom in harsh cruelty it has taken away; I address myself to all those who detached from their mother country, have to fight even for the holy treasure of their language, who are persecuted and tortured for their loyalty to the fatherland, and who now, with poignant emotion, long for the hour which will permit them to return to the heart of their faithful mother; I address myself to all those and I know that they will understand me.
>
> "Only he who has felt in his own skin what it means to be German, deprived of the right to belong to his cherished fatherland, can measure the deep longing which burns at all times in the hearts of children separated from their mother country. It torments those whom it fills and denies them contentment and happiness until the gates of their father's house opens, and in the common Reich, common blood gains peace and tranquillity."

Obviously German Christians understood the religion to authorize such feelings.

The above aspects of the Mystical Body, the Gospel teaching that money is the root of all evil, and the ideal of all men working for Christ in return for distinctions Christ chooses to give, are understood in many Christian nations to indicate that the ideal economy is one in which all men work for the same man as his arms, as cogs in his machine. Since religious should view themselves as working for Christ twenty-four hours a day in a place in which all real and personal property is owned by the community or by the top man, the ideal national economy should be the same. Hence government should own the means of production. The result is that this employer would have great powers to hold people down because he has the say as to what anyone should have and how he should enjoy it. The aspect in effect holds as ideal the position of a child to his parents. The child does chores around the house in return for a bicycle or other reward of the parents' choosing. The parent chooses the chore, the reward, and how it will be enjoyed. He retains total control.

The Gospel teaching and its interpretation in Roman Catholicism and the Greek Orthodox Church thus provide authorization for the Fascist and Communist types of economy. This interpretation also obscures recognition that a society in which men work for money and pay their taxes in money is one that insures the greatest possible amount of personal freedom of choice of occupation, of place of work, school, home, neighborhood, furniture, use of leisure time, and so on, to he who desires such freedom. Not only freedom of choice but where, when, and how to choose, freedom to make one's own decisions without having to justify them to anyone.

In summary, the Gospel message and the Mystical Body are understood to authorize an economic system in which one's interests are one with one's employer. As the Apostles and disciples supposedly were with Christ and priests and nuns are with Christ. Historically this understanding provided authorization for the company town, in which the mill owner also owns the workers' homes and stores, which he rents to employees. Such projects have usually been ruined by the individualism of the employees. They want to remodel the buildings and the yards, to own the property so they can mortgage it, come and go as they please without others knowing it, and so on. Receiving one's wages in the form of a house, bigger or smaller or otherwise different from that desired, is seen as an erosion of personal freedom. Receiving one's wages in the form of a bed in a barrackslike monastery and a promise of a reward in the next world is a much greater erosion of personal freedom.

The Mystical Body of Christ provides authorization for a political system in which there is no warrant to be a citizen independent from the requirements of the top man or the nation. Education therein is defined as that which serves the purposes of the state. And everyone should be satisfied leading a frugal existence with a shabby line of consumer goods, while vast resources are poured into the military, because one's personal life should be oriented to the purpose of the top man. Everyone should also be satisfied with a bureaucracy that renders personal services to all comers. Just as it is disloyal to express dissatisfaction with Christ, it is disloyal to express dissatisfaction with the personal services of these government agencies.

Seven

Abstraction: Law Becomes a Person; Inalienable Rights Become Alienable; Whatever the Top Man Permits

In this chapter we deal with the abstract concept of rights. These are of very ancient understanding in Judaism. As is the rest of the Hebrew Law, these rights are God-given, no man can take them away. In British and American law, this understanding is expressed in the statement, "Men are endowed by their Creator with certain inalienable rights." A right is that to which one has a just claim in law.

In Exodus, the Hebrew Law states that if the servant is mistreated by his master in certain ways, the servant has the right to go free. The understanding is that the servant has inalienable rights to life and liberty and to protect those rights he can go free. He has the right not to be mutilated by another person. But before Exodus is the understanding attached to Abraham's sacrifice his son. God's messenger stays Abraham's hand and Abraham offers instead a lamb, because it is the Law of the God of the Hebrews that human sacrifice is wrong. The understanding is that it is wrong, because men are endowed with inalienable rights to life. A God who endows men with inalienable rights to life cannot be worshipped by a human sacrifice. (And therefore the sacrifice of the Mass cannot be a worship of the God of the Hebrews.)

By this lesson of Abraham, the Hebrew religion differentiated itself from pagan religions around it. For example, in the idol Moloch, there was a small furnace in which newborn babies were roasted to death as a sacrifice to this god. Other pagan customs called for self-mutilation by the religious adherent to prove his love and loyalty to his pagan god. This often took the form of sexual self-mutilation. However, it is the Law of the God of the Hebrews that such mutilation is wrong as is celibacy, nonviolent self-mutilation. The rite of circumcision is performed by the Jew to indicate that he understands and accepts this rule of law.

By 200 B.C. the Hebrew Law as expressed in Exodus through Deuteronomy had evolved into something more humane than that of Moses' time: it recognized the rights of the accused, the right to trial by jury, and capital punishment was almost non-existent in recognition of one's inalienable right to life.

In Christianity, this Law becomes Christ or His authority on Earth. What becomes of inalienable rights? The apostles and disciples, being Jews and members of the Jewish community, must have been aware of their rights as Jews understood them at that time. But this is not what comes through the Gospels. There, the followers of Christ are represented as not being the least bit aware of any such concept as a right. Also, Christ's trial before Jewish authorities is a misrepresentation of the almost complete nonexistence of capital punishment under the Hebrew Law at that time. The effect of these misrepresentations is to obscure recognition that one's inalienable rights disappear with the Christian departure from Judaism. The belief that Christ was put on earth as a human sacrifice for the redemption of the world is an indication that men, as Christ, have been given no inalienable rights to life. But Christ, by being a Jew, is saying that He and all men do have inalienable rights.

In Christian belief, Christ's parents raised their Son for human sacrifice, for torment, mutilation, and death in order to redeem the world. His mother, Mary, according to belief, knew from His conception that she would raise him for these purposes. The belief provides authorization in the political sphere for the view that the home exists to provide sons for sacrifice, mutilation, and death in war as cannon fodder. Mary is one who would allow her most private parts to be invaded so she would be the mother of God, holding as ideal a lack of awareness of the right of privacy.

Christ is recognized as having known the inmost thoughts of His followers. They are members of a society in which no one has the right of privacy and in which no one has the right to question or disagree with Him. Those who did so such as the Pharisees were excoriated. Christ said, "You are either with me or against me."

The above themes, we have seen in previous chapters, are Christian understandings forced on events. These understandings are seen as authorizing religious communities of celibate men and women in which the individuals have no right to privacy, or right to protect themselves from such nonviolent mutilation. Under the Hebrew Law these people have the inalienable right to go free at once. A Roman hierarchy whose membership is drawn from celibates, is, therefore, one by definition made up of persons who recognize no inalienable rights, who recognize that everyone's privacy should be invaded in this fashion. These understandings authorize the sacrament of Confession in which one's most secret trangressions must be confessed to a priest who is an agent of the top man, Jesus Christ. And for the vows of obedience and poverty that religious take, which preclude any sort of a private life in the religious life. Total openness of one's life to one's superiors is the ideal.

It would appear that the inalienable rights in Judaism became in Christianity whatever rights or liberties the Man who is the Law permits. Thus inalienable rights became alienable. One's liberties are like a sailor's shore liberty: time off for good behavior.

The liberty of the individual disappears as Law becomes a Man or is set aside by Him. Thus Christian disciplinary procedure calls for one to be assumed guilty until proved innocent, as in the courts of the Roman Church today. As the Jews are guilty for having crucified Christ, even though Jews as individuals have never been given a free trial for this "crime." As each person born into the world is guilty of the Original Sin of Adam and Eve, without a trial, as all Christians are guilty before Christ, without a trial. All because in Christian belief, the Law that says men are endowed with inalienable rights, such as to a free trial, has been set aside. As has the Law that says all men are created equal. Those people who are above stated as having been created guilty without a trial, are not equal to those created innocent in Christianity by the sacraments.

In both Christianity and Judaism all law is God-given. In Judaism this means that because God is not and cannot become man, His Law is immutable by men. In Christianity this means that because God became Man, this same Law can be set aside by the God-Man and His vicar, His authority on Earth.

As Law becomes a Person and the individual becomes one with that person in the Mystical Body, it was understood in the Roman Church that Christians should be one with Christ in their desire for rights, freedom, and liberty. Such desire is understood to be for the freedom and liberty of the Church to fulfill its functions: not a desire for individual freedom as understood in the English-speaking nations. Thus one is inescapably a part of a body. The Roman Catholic masses were, until recently, concluded with a prayer for the conversion of Russia which petitioned "the freedom, liberty and exultation of Holy Mother Church. . ."

This is a militaristic conception of mankind. "A division breaks out to freedom," means that it is rejoined to its supply line and the remainder of its army. It never means that the men are sent home to live free lives.

This theme of freedom of the body politic is prominent in Communist ideology. The People's Free Republics of Poland, East Germany and Czechoslovakia are each free as a body politic from capitalist exploitation. Individual freedom is never understood to be permitted. Thus these nations were "liberated" by the Red Army in 1945. The theme is also very prominent in Hitler's writing. He speaks of "the freedom and independence of the Fatherland," "peoples without honor have sooner or later lost their freedom and independence."

Thus members of the Mystical Body do not have individual rights, as for example, the Roman Church's teaching on the rights of parents to educate their children. Parents do have this right, but as agents of the Church, they have the duty to send their children to Catholic schools.

Recognizing that inalienable rights are central to Judaism, what might account for this lack of awareness of rights in Christianity in addition to the other reasons mentioned? In Christianity, everything else is visible, so if men are endowed with rights, how is it that no one can see them? The burden was on he who claims inalienable rights to prove that he has such or that there is such a thing. The authorities could produce a visible God who is the Law, a Mystical Body, and other visible abstractions. Constitutional governments have foundered over the past centuries for just these reasons. Rights are not visible as kings and dictators are and as God supposedly is. If God is visible, why aren't the rights that he endowed men with visible also? The God who has no image has endowed men with rights and liberties, which also have no image. Also awareness of rights evolves out of the boy-girl relationship. The weaker sex has inalienable rights with respect to the stronger sex, with respect to her parents, with respect to anyone else.

Having defined the religious difference above, let us consider the Christian beliefs below.

1. Before Christ, these are the alternative Christian beliefs:

a) The Hebrew religion was valid. This means that men were endowed with certain God-given inalienable rights. The development of understanding of such rights was and is an ongoing process.

b) The Hebrew religion was valid but men were endowed only with rights that were alienable. Jews, therefore, must have misunderstood their own Bible, as did the Anglo-Saxons who built British and American law. This position in effect holds that the Hebrew religion never was valid. Therefore, Christianity is a valid religion built on one that never was valid, which is an untenable position.

2.   With the coming of Christ, the Christian religion became valid and is valid today.

At this point in time, inalienable rights became alienated. Presumably this point in time is at the moment of conception of Christ in the womb of Mary, because this event alienates Mary's inalienable right of privacy. But why is Christ still practicing Judaism until the Last Supper when the religion became invalid at the moment of His conception? Again it is clear that the Christian interpretation is a meaning forced on the text.

3.   After Christ, these are the alternative Christian beliefs:

a) The Hebrew religion is still valid but obsolete. This alternative Christian belief holds that men are and are not endowed with inalienable rights in the same instant in time. This cannot be a valid belief because it is inherently contradictory. This belief secondly holds that the idea of inalienable rights is valid but obsolete. Millions of English-speaking people would instantly disagree. They know of nothing obsolete about it.

b) The Hebrew religion is no longer valid. This means that men are no longer endowed with inalienable rights. Many millions, some of whom fought in one of two world wars for such rights, would instantly disagree.

By now a pattern has become obvious. The Hebrew understanding of their Bible is far more sensible to the modern common man than the Christian interpretation. Because Christians have so completely ignored Judaism, they are unaware of their predicament of having made a departure to a concept of the rights of man (which concept is that men effectively have *no* rights) that millions hate, that millions have fought against and died fighting, because this concept is so obviously used to hold people down. The Christian understanding is a meaning forced on the Hebrew account and it does not fit; it cannot be made to fit. And it is no longer a mystery as to why Christianity cannot be reconciled with Judaism.

Christ and His Apostles constitute a society in which men

are not conscious of their rights. The celibate clergy constitutes another such society. These societies provide authorization for a political system whose leader should know everything that each citizen is doing and can require that every aspect of each citizen's life, even the most intimate, be done as he requires, which is a meaning of the vow of celibacy; whose leaders should rightly keep dossiers or otherwise spy on citizens. In such a society it is right for children to report to political leaders the transgressions of their parents, ultimately because the state is a parent also.

The concept of property is as a bundle of rights: the right to work the land, to build a house on it, to live in it as if it is one's castle, and so on. Without the concept of rights there is no concept of right of property. Hence, in Soviet Russia, there is no private property, nor is there any in the celibate religious communities. Even one's body is not private property. These beliefs authorize the kind of society that is satirized by Orwell in *1984*. Big Brother, the political leader, watches you at all times, even in your home. He is always present. Just as it is right for one's parents to know everything that goes on in one's mind, one should tell the truth and the whole truth to them at all times.

Rule through history has been, with few exceptions, the rule of tyranny. With the Industrial Revolution, political authorities were provided with new technical means for abuse of their power. This means has been used to gain total control over the individual citizen so that he could be exploited in military adventures, for the purpose of gaining more control over more people and ultimately the world. This has been the pattern of development of the modern totalitarian state. But this tyranny exists ultimately because the concepts of rights, liberties, freedom and equality of all men are purely religious concepts and unless one accepts these concepts as part of his religion, one need not accept them at all.

Hence even in America this concept of rights is not well understood. There is current the idea that since Negroes score lower on intelligence tests than whites, Negroes do not have rights equal to whites. As if the I.Q. test would prove or disprove that men have such rights.

Eight

Religion as a Thought System

In the previous chapters, I have shown that the Hebrew mathematically expressible concepts are abstract and invisible as are Arabic numeral and modern mathematical concepts; the Christian counterpart in each case is concrete and visible as are Roman numeral concepts. The two religions overlap in the person of Christ. The Christian should follow and imitate Him in those ways that have a visible expression: by accepting one or another of the visible authorities that rule in His name.

To follow and imitate Christ in an abstract invisible sense is, on the contrary, to become a Jew as Christ was: to accept rule by the abstract invisible Hebrew Law in the religious and political spheres. It is to accept common sense, as mathematics is common sense, in all spheres. Thus Christians and Jews agree on the common sense understandings that are expressed in modern mathematics, science, and technology, but they disagree on the common sense understandings in the religious sphere and in spheres influenced by religion. Jews hold to the common sense understanding that infinity cannot become limited, abstraction cannot become a person, and so on. Christians maintain their irrational understanding apparently by keeping closed minds on the subject. The irrational understanding is like an island in the Christian mind surrounded by a sea of common sense.

The irrational understanding impales Christians in totalitarian nations on the horns of the dilemma because they must accept the visible authority in the religious sphere, it must be right to accept the same in the political sphere. This is acceptance of one—perhaps benevolent dictator or another. The dilemma is false because it is irrational and ignores a perfectly common

111

sense alternative that has no visible expression: rule by the Hebrew Law. It has been noted in previous chapters how completely Christians have ignored the common sense of Judaism.

Recognizing that the first Christians were Jews, we ask why Christians have so completely ignored Judaism? Another way of phrasing the question is, why doesn't the sea of common sense sweep away this island of irrationality in the minds of Christians?

It would appear that this island of irrationality was created in the ignorance of Roman times, which ignorance conceived the gods as persons, because the mathematics and science of that day was not sufficiently developed. God as a Person was understood to authorize celibacy. It will be seen below that the island of irrationality corresponds to that area of thinking that is prohibited by the vows of celibacy.

One reason Christians have so completely ignored Judaism is that they apparently read the Bible distracted by the spectacle of Christ's resurrection and ascension, the entertainment of Christ's miracles, the violence of Christ crucified, and the crime of the Jews, which are similar to the distractions offered on television. The Law is ignored because it became the distractions on becoming Flesh in Christ. The Gospels provide distraction because it is needed by those who dare not think of the opposite sex lest vows of celibacy be broken. This need for distraction has been adopted by the ordinary Christian man and can be seen everywhere in radio, television, and other superficial entertainment. By comparison, great literature and great music are ignored. Thus, one does not read a book, one waits until it is made into a movie, a spectacle, a distraction. In Judaism, knowledge of good and evil begins by recognizing the nature of distraction and that such in the opposite sex serves that person's purposes. The Gospels are distractions from the Hebrew Law and serve the purposes of the religious and, therefore, the political authorities.

Thus, our first reason why Christians are so totally distracted from seeing the Hebrew Law must be that the Christian religion actually is the opium of the people, that Christians are actually locked within a framework, that the religion traps its adherents in the limited rational behavior of an emotional trap as drug addicts are trapped into running in circles around drugs. This is because our understanding of Christ has come down to us through a celibate clergy, who are trapped within their vows and whose romantic thoughts of Christ are a substitute for romantic thoughts of the opposite sex.

Our second reason, closely related to our first reason, is that in love between the sexes the other person visibly expresses his or her invisible thoughts, abstractions, and it is essential to the relationship to actually understand such thoughts. In celibate love, Christ is visible and in the Gospels He visibly expresses His thoughts, abstractions, as a Jew, but it has never been essential to understand such thoughts. Otherwise Christians would not have monumentally ignored Judaism. Thus Christ is seen by Christians as a visible entity only, a projection, a glorification of one's self, a statue. Christ is whatever one wants Him to be. It is not essential to actually understand such thoughts because there is no actual relationship or partnership between the Christian, celibate or otherwise, and Christ. Thus again, Christ as Christians see Him is a meaning forced on the text to serve someone's purposes. Christ as Christians see Him is the expression of Christians' need to use someone.

Our third reason is that one's relationship with the opposite sex tends to influence one's relationship to anyone. The vows of celibacy require that the celibate see the opposite sex only as a visible entity (and not too much of that even), that he not dwell on that person's thoughts as a basis for her behavior, least of all the thoughts of the women who passionately assault him. Thus, these men see Christ and all persons in the same fashion.

The above is not to say that the celibate clergy ignore abstraction. It is well-known that many are outstanding mathematicians, lawyers, etc.

Another reason why Christians have totally ignored Judaism is their emotional involvement with Christ, one aspect of which is the status of being better than those who crucified Christ and another aspect of which is, "Believe in the Lord Jesus Christ and you will be saved." To actually consider Judaism is, thus, to renounce one's status and to reject salvation. Those who conceive themselves of high status, of having a social position, are easily made jealous and irrational if that status is threatened. Hence, in the face of the status of the Jews as Chosen, such people need an island of irrationality of which they are on top.

Another reason why is that Christian themes hold as ideal an unquestioning attitude toward one's faith, even unto death. For example, Christian belief is that Christ was placed on earth as a human sacrifice for the redemption of mankind: He is seen as locked within a system for which there was no escape but torment and death as a public spectacle. The system was established before His birth. There was nothing He could do to change the purposes for which He was placed on earth. (He is, therefore, without inalienable rights to life and liberty.) All men should imitate Christ as the Lamb of God, sacrificed on the cross. From the vows of celibacy, obedience, and poverty that religious in some Christian orders take in perpetuity, there is no escape but death. In such a life, all that most people hold dear is sacrificed. Individuals live out their lives completely subject to their superiors. Such vows are judged by some to be destructive of the individual's personality. Christianity provides authorization for total obedience because Christ is seen as totally obedient to the will of another Person, His Father in Heaven. And this religion has come down to us through a clergy controlled in this fashion.

Another reason why Christians have so totally ignored Judaism is the ideal of viewing things as a child that is a well-known Christian theme. Christians learn such views as children and do not unlearn them. Celibacy is virtuous for children. The child's rationality is limited because he cannot be permitted to question or investigate everything or to act freely. The child is typically oriented to spectacle and entertainment, the visibly expressible aspects of anything rather than the abstract. If all men should be as children, then the religious authorities should do whatever is necessary to stay in control, as adults should stay in charge of children.

Another reason why Christians have ignored Judaism is the ideal of the Christian as a soldier of Christ. The soldier is not to question, "Ours is not to reason why, ours is just to do and die," even unto death. He may find himself locked within a system from which the only escape is perhaps spectacular torment and death on the battlefield. He has no control over his situation. He is to follow as sheep to slaughter. Other Christian beliefs assist the Christian in not questioning his faith even unto death. These are the beliefs in the forgiveness of sins, the resurrection of the body, life everlasting, plenary indulgence, and Holy Eucharist. If one's sins can be forgiven and one's body resurrected intact for life everlasting, then one cannot really be killed or mutilated in war. If one's main concern in this world should be life after death, then mutilation and death don't really matter, and questioning one's faith is an idle waste of time.

Another expression of the limited rationality of "Ours is not to reason why . . ." is that summed up in the words of Christ: "Feed my lambs, feed my sheep," and "There shall be one fold and one Shepherd," in which men are referred to as sheep, which, like Christ, are eventually slaughtered. The theme occurs again in the words of Christ: "I shall make thee fishers of men." Men should be caught like fish? in a net from which there is no escape but to be slaughtered and eaten. (This herd theme can be seen as providing authorization for herd unity and herd homogeneity among men, which ideas are Hitler's)

Thus, this island of irrationality of nonsense that has been defined as existing in the Christian mind is a sense of being ideally a public spectacle locked within a trap or framework that ultimately leads to a tragic end. This is a theme of ancient Greek plays, for example, *Electra,* in which the heroine is driven to incest. And this is also the homosexual condition. Those inflicted with this mental disease, from which they find no escape, are driven to antisocial behavior of the worst sort, and eventually to imprisonment. The vows of celibacy make a public spectacle of reducing the celibate to the homosexual condition. Any sexual expression is to be fearfully punished because vows have thereby been broken. There are many homosexual themes in Christianity: the religious and political romanticism mentioned earlier; the lack of love and affection between the sexes and lack of insight into personalities that pervades the Gospels; the idea that the greatest love story ever told is Christ laying down his life for his fellowman. These themes glorify those who are used: the homosexual is one who was used for sexual purposes as a child, perhaps spectacularly, by the parent or other adult. The religious or political romantic and the celibate are also used for sexual purposes by the Mystical Body or the body politic.

This sense of being a public spectacle locked within a trap that leads to a tragic end presumably received so much emphasis in the Gospels because of its great appeal to slaves, soldiers and others in the Roman Empire, raised for a specific spectacular destructive purpose, of being tormented to death. He who is a soldier is raised for death in battle is a popular understanding. Some slaves were raised to be male or female prostitutes or raised so that the authorities and spectators could have the fun of seeing them bullied and tormented in the arena. From some gladiatorial fights, the only way out was death. In other events, slaves could run in circles to escape being eaten by lions or other beasts.

Recognizing that this island of irrationality had its origin in Roman times and persists today in the celibate mind and those dominated by a celibate clergy, we can see that the decline of Christianity since the Renaissance is an expression of the decline of this island of irrationality before the seas of common sense. The revival of Greek learning, the introduction of Arabic numerals, the development of modern science and technology have brought about this decline by giving the common man confidence in his use of common sense.

Thus this mathematically expressible religious difference is that the truths of Judaism are a rigorous common sense development from self-evident truths as, for example, Euclidean geometry is such from axioms and postulates.

Having defined this mathematically expressible difference, let us consider what follows in the religious sphere.

This sense of being a public spectacle locked within a trap that leads to a tragic end, that is such an important theme of the Christian religion, is now the situation of the entire world. It is expressed in the motto of a well-known British political movement of the 1960s: "Better Red Than Dead." We are locked within a world in which we have the choice of enslavement by Communism or death in nuclear war. Or perhaps peaceful coexistence for a time. The worship of Christ, the Prince of Peace, has created this problem. Those who worship Christ will not question the irrational aspects of their religion, which aspects are the subjects of these chapters, because they feel that they will lose eternal salvation by such an exercise of their rationality. But what would actually happen is that they will find their way to Judaism and hence to religious and political freedom for the entire Christian world.

It is a limited rationality that does not question the present world situation of Christianity divided into denominations, many of whom hold contradictory beliefs. Some hundreds of millions of people must be in error in these most cherished beliefs because any two contradictory beliefs can't be true, and because few Christian truths are acceptable to all men as ultimate truths. But Christians ought to be ready at all times to die for their faith in Christ rather than to deny Him. The beliefs should not be questioned even in the face of death.

This limited rationality in Christianity provides authorization for a similar view in the political sphere. The world is divided into many nations, several of which hold contradictory foreign policies. Some millions of people must be wrong. In the two world wars millions of Christians were willing to lay down their lives for what they thought was right in opposition to millions of others who believed that something contradictory was right. But just as these questions are insoluble between Christian denominations, they are insoluble between Christian nations. Only world rule of law can provide a means to settle such disputes. However, the worse the world situation becomes, the more people are driven to prayer and thoughts of Jesus the Savior, and the farther they go from solving the world's problems. It is a vicious circle. It is behavior without a self-correcting (feedback) mechanism and it is behavior limited to following visibly expressible entities.

Certain species of grazing animals and social insects exhibit this behavior because they are limited to such by their instincts. To us the behavior looks ridiculous. In mill movement, the herd stampedes in a circle, each member following the one in front of him all around one center. All but the inner and outer members see all other members traveling along with him. All apparently think they are going some place. Eventually they will wear themselves out and perhaps members in the interior of the mill will be crushed. The animals are locked within their mental framework of limited rationality, from which there is no escape except total exhaustion and death. Or perhaps a thunderstorm will distract them.

In the behavior of ants or bees the same pattern can be observed. Swarms of these insects can be set to follow a circular path, like the herd of grazing animals, until they are exhausted or die, because they are unable to question their situation. Christianity provides authorization for the same behavior by holding it ideal not to question one's religious situation and then correct it.

Mill movement is the behavior of organisms without feedback. No grazing animal or insect caught in it can do what is required: step outside the crowd and point out the error, as the Jewish prophets of old did for their people. Thus the world is marching in circles through two world wars and the Cold War toward world destruction. No person can speak out against the leadership of Christ or the Christian beliefs that create this behavior because then that person becomes an anti-Christ.

Having defined this aspect of the religious difference, let us consider the Christian beliefs below:

1.   Before Christ, these are the alternative Christian beliefs:

a)   The Hebrew religion was valid. This is to say that Christians agree that Judaism is a rational thought system of abstract concepts in agreement with Arabic numeral mathematics. It was developed by common sense from God-given laws through the centuries. The Hebrew Bible is an account of this development before the Christian Era.

b) The Hebrew religion was valid but the Christian religion was valid also. The latter however had not yet been revealed to be true. As said in previous chapters, Christian and Hebrew beliefs contradict each other. So this Christian belief that both were valid cannot be valid.

2. With the coming of Christ the Christian religion became valid and is valid today.

This means that at some time in Christ's life, probably at the time of His birth of a virgin, several common sense truths of Judaism became no longer true. This belief raises difficult questions about the Hebrew religion Christ practiced. The Gospels tell of Christ as a Child in the temple applying His common sense in understanding the Law. If Christ is God at birth, and His message is the new religion in which one can no longer use one's common sense in several aspects, in which one now instead must believe, why does He contradict Himself by using His common sense in the old religion, when this religion is already invalid? Secondly, why is it that His Jewish followers do not question Him on this point? If one should imitate Christ, why not imitate Him as a Jew and apply one's common sense in matters religious? Recognizing that His followers were Jews, why aren't they represented as doing this?

The Acts of the Apostles answers these questions. Christianity was simply a movement within Judaism until Paul, in disagreement with Peter, decided to admit the Gentiles without their going through Judaism. The movement soon became engulfed by new converts and the religion was converted into a belief system in agreement with the old Greek and Roman Pagan mythology. But this departure was not authorized by Peter, the rock on which Christ built His church. Nor was it authorized by Christ who said, "Not one title shall pass from the Law until all things be fulfilled."

3.   After Christ these are the alternative Christian beliefs:

a) The Hebrew religion is still valid but obsolete. This would hold it right but obsolete to use one's common sense, as Arabic numeral mathematics is common sense, in these religious matters.

b) The Hebrew religion is no longer valid. This means that it was once right to use one's common sense and the Hebrew Law in the religious sphere but it is not now. Though the common people of the world must orient themselves to rule in the religious and political spheres as a solution to world problems, it is not valid to do so. The world supposedly should resign itself to destruction by nuclear war.

Because Christians have so completely ignored Judaism, they are in the predicament of having made a departure to a religion that holds people down by keeping them from using their common sense to solve their problems and by making them feel inadequate to solve these religious mysteries. And they regard this as an improvement.

What happened with the origin of Christianity is that the concepts of Judaism "evolved" into the concepts of Roman militarism. With these concepts, Rome conquered the world, and Christians have conquered much of the world since the Crusades. These concepts obviously have immense war-making potential. Some observers of the modern state of Israel see the same "evolution" happening. The military demands are so great that they are becoming more important than the demands of the religion, and Judaism is being replaced by militarism. Some Americans think that the Constitution and Bill of Rights is being weakened by the demands of military necessity.

Thus one must believe that Judaism evolved into Christianity, that it is a mystery as to why the God of the Hebrews who made men free evolved into a God who can be used to hold people down, because to turn away from the militarism of Christianity is to invite defeat in war. Thus perhaps no Jewish nation can be established permanently, unless every nation is Jewish. And perhaps no free nation can be permanent unless every nation is free, because no peoples want to be overrun and scattered over the world as have the Jews through history.

Let us consider what follows from the above defined religious difference in the political sphere, to the extent we have not done so already.

Because this aspect of Christianity authorizes a thought system based on concepts other than common sense self-evident truths, it provides authorization for such a political thought system also. Hence the widespread acceptance in Christian nations of the philosophies of Nazism, Fascism, and Russian Communism. Each has its nonsensical story authorizing a certain political system. Just as one must belive in the Lord Jesus Christ in order to be saved, those who do not believe these political stories are herded into concentration camps where they are also not saved. These nonsense stories have such wide appeal, because nothing can be proved right or wrong to those who believe such as that infinity can be limited, abstraction personified, and men can be perfect. The leaders of these political movements need these nonsense philosophies in order to create thought systems that provide a basis for totalitarian rule. Since the citizen is not sensible enough to see for himself that the nonsense is sensible, he must be told what to think. He must be controlled by party members who do believe in the political philosophy and are willing to die for their faith. He should rightly be yelled at, forced, and threatened as if he is a dumb animal (such as a sheep) and bribed with a promise of a worker's paradise and a heaven hereafter.

If it is right in the religious sphere for followers to live out their lives never questioning these matters or never thinking about sex as does the celibate, then it is seen as right for political leaders to bring about such effects in subordinates also by brainwashing. This is a process utilizing drugs and psychiatry for the purpose of gaining complete control over recalcitrant individuals. If it is right for Christ to completely surrender to His father's will, then it is right to force those who profess to imitate Christ to completely surrender also.

By these Christian beliefs, men are raised like game cocks for the sport of international slaughter. Just as slaves, at the bottom of the Roman world, could be publicly and spectacularly expended for the entertainment of authorities in the Colosseum, one senses in Christianity the idea that the common man can be expended in war, exploited economically, and otherwise mutilated for the service and entertainment of authorities religious and political.

An aspect of Christian belief is Christ's Second Coming. The previous pages indicate that Judaism cannot validly evolve into Christianity and that Judaism has an immensely important message to the world. Recognizing such, there is no reason to think that if Christ did return, that He would do other than practice present day Judaism and reject Christianity.

Nine

Conclusion

It is the thesis of this book that the only common sense solution to world problems is for Christians to admit to themselves that the Christian departure is without validity and that the Jews are right after all. It is clear to the common man that the military problems of the world will not be solved by the military. This book attempts to make it clear that these military problems were and are created and are authorized by the militarism inherent in the Christian religion. Thus the only way to rid the world of militarism is for all Christians nations together to abandon Christianity in favor of Judaism. This would also offer a realistic option to the Israeli Jews to move out of Palestine.

We have seen that Judaism provides a means by which an old American dream can be attained. The dream is that the principles of the American Revolution would someday be spread around the world, which idea is expressed in that self-evident truth that *all* men are created equal. However, this is not to suggest that Americanism or Britishism can be equated with Judaism. Judaism could never accommodate that violence which has characterized Americanism, that arrogance which has characterized British rule, or that rapacious disregard for the laws of nature which has characterized Christian behavior for centuries. Nor could it accommodate that indifference to the history of ideas and to any history which understands British and American law to be purely an invention of English-speaking peoples. But this is to suggest that these *isms* could be replaced by Judaism, which not only has political and legal aspects but is also a religion.

The implications of world-wide establishment of Jewish rule

of Law are so manifold that they can only begin to be listed: Judaism provides a direction by which the human race can emerge from its undereducated, underfed, underclothed, undersheltered, overpopulated, and overworked condition, because it is now overentertained with mythology. Judaism could also provide a working basis for an end to the Cold War, at least between the Free World and Russia; for the expansion of such free trade areas as the European Common Market; for the destruction of that last bastion of population limitation, the Roman Church; for a positive urge to conserve the world's natural resources; for an end to the Middle East crisis; for replacement of the Continental Civil law with Common law; and for an end to militarism. Each of these is appropriately the subject of several books.

Bibliography

Adorno, T. W., *et al. The Authoritarian Personality.* Vols. I-II, New York: John Wiley & Sons, Inc., 1964.

Bokser, Ben Zion. *Judaism and the Christian Predicament.* New York: Alfred A. Knopf, Inc., 1967.

Buchheim, Hans. *Totalitarian Rule.* Middletown, Connecticut: Wesleyan University Press, 1968.

Bury, J. B. *History of the Papacy in the 19th Century.* Schocken Books, Inc., 1964.

Fine, Sidney. *Laissez Faire and the General Welfare State.* Ann Arbor, Michigan: University of Michigan Press, 1956.

Galbraith, J. K. *The Affluent Society.* Boston: Houghton Mifflin Company, 1958.

Golding, William. *Lord of the Flies.* New York: Coward-Mc-Cann, Inc., 1962.

Hayek, Friedrich A. *The Road to Serfdom.* Chicago: University of Chicago Press, 1945.

Hertzberg, Arthur, Editor. *Judaism.* New York: George Braziller, 1962.

Hilbersiemer, Ludwig K. *The Nature of Cities.* Chicago: Paul Theobald and Company, 1955.

Hilberg, Raul. *The Destruction of the European Jews.* Chicago: Quadrangle Books, 1967.

Hitler, Adolf. *Mein Kampf.* Boston: Houghton Mifflin Company, 1943.

Hofstader, Richard. *Anti-Intellectualism in American Life.* New York: Alfred A. Knopf, Inc., 1963.

Isaac, Jules. *The Teaching of Contempt.* New York: McGraw-Hill Book Company, Inc., 1965.

Jefferson, Thomas. *The Jefferson Bible.* New York: Clarkson N. Potter, Inc., 1964.

Kirby, *et al. Engineering in History.* New York: McGraw-Hill Book Company, Inc., 1956.

Kline, Morris. *Mathematics in Western Culture.* New York: Oxford University Press, 1953.

Laqueur, Walter Z. *Young Germany.* New York: Basic Books, Inc., 1962.

Lewy, Guenter. *The Catholic Church and Nazi Germany.* New York: McGraw-Hill Book Company, Inc., 1964.

Milosz, Czeslaw. *The Captive Mind.* New York: Alfred A. Knopf, Inc., 1953.

O'Dea, Thomas F. *American Catholic Dilemma.* New York: Mentor Omega Books, 1962.

Rubenstein, Richard L. *After Auschwitz.* Indianapolis, Indiana: The Bobbs-Merrill Company, Inc., 1966.

Sachar, Abram Leon. *A History of the Jews.* New York: Alfred A. Knopf, Inc., 1966.

Sandmel, Samuel. *We Jews and You Christians.* Philadelphia: J. B. Lippincott Company, 1964.

de Santillana, Giorgio. *The Crime of Galileo.* Chicago: University of Chicago Press, 1955.

Schneider, Peter. *The Dialogue of Christians and Jews.* New York: Seabury Press, 1966.

Shirer, William L. *The Rise and Fall of the Third Reich.* Greenwich, Connecticut: Fawcett Publications, Inc., 1960.

Singer, Charles, *et al. A History of Technology.* Vols. I-V, New York: Oxford University Press, 1954.

Spengler, Oswald. *The Decline of the West.* New York: Alfred A. Knopf, Inc., 1962.

Toynbee, Arnold J. *A Study of History.* Abridgment by D. C. Somervell. New York: Oxford University Press, 1946.

Weber, Max. *The Protestant Ethic and the Spirit of Capitalism.* translated by Talcott Parsons, New York: Charles Scribner's Sons, 1958.

Wells, H. G. *The Outline of History.* Vols. I-II, Garden City, New York: Garden City Books, 1953.

Zahn, Gordon. *In Solitary Witness.* New York: Holt, Rinehart and Winston, Inc., 1964.